The Un-Tended Altar

BY

JEN MCCARTY

The Untended Altar

How to work with the Spiritual Vortex in your home.

By Jen McCarty

REVIEWS FOR THE UNTENDED ALTAR

"Merely a handful of words into the first page, I was struck by a potent flurry of energy throughout my crown chakra. Lightning bolt after lightning bolt, as I ingested each of the first few chapters. Such was the extremely deep level at which every syllable resonated. This remarkable book is doubtlessly the motivational kick up the backside I have been needing to get my house in order, and steer me forwards on my journey. Thank you so much." ***Mari A.***

"Before reading The Untended Altar, I was struggling to push forward in my spiritual journey but not sure what my next move would be. This little gem fell into my lap like all things with divine timing. Jen McCarty is such a rich resource of profound wisdom and a true living guide for the future human. The Untended Altar serves to bring the unconscious into the physical and teaches you where to start. It was something I didn't know that I needed but now can't imagine living without." ***Amy M.***

"I have had the privilege of reading the first 5 chapters of "The Untended Altar" by Jen Mccarty. It spoke volumes to my soul! Sharing her unique experience and insight.

By Jen McCarty

The Untended Altar

A Reminder, Remembrance and Invitation to realise that polishing our internal lives to reflect our highest potential is so needed. As with any divinely inspired works, it will speak to readers on the level of their individual journey as it has to me and my particular circumstances. Looking forward to the release of the book to see what further Gems are in there." **Liberty H.**

By Jen McCarty

Proofreading and Front/Back Matter Copy Editing: Zoe

Book Front Cover Artist: Jen McCarty

First Print Edition 21/12/2022

By Jen McCarty

Disclaimer Notice:

Although the author has made every effort to ensure that the information in this book was correct at time of press, the author does not assume and hereby disclaims any liability to any party for any loss, damage, or disruption caused by errors or omissions, whether such errors or omissions result from negligence, accident, or any other cause.

This book is not intended as a substitute for the medical advice of physicians. The reader should regularly consult a physician in matters relating to his/her health and particularly with respect to any symptoms that may require diagnosis or medical attention.

All of the information that I share has been received directly through my own access to the Akashic Records. Nothing that I share is regurgitated information; it is all based on downloads that I have personally received. It is so important that as you are reading these words, you exercise your own discernment and only take on as truth that which resonates for you as truth. If something does not feel true to you, then that is correct; so please do honour that.

By Jen McCarty

The Untended Altar

Regardless of where you are on your spiritual path, whether you be a beginner or a seasoned explorer into the deepest mysteries of existence, the words in this book will awaken memories in you that have long been sleeping - memories of your true and abiding divinity.

The words are organised in such a way that it can be likened to light language and light codes. These words transcend the boundaries of time and space and align immediately with your heart's consciousness. The key to Christ Consciousness is through the heart.

In love and eternal light, Jen and the White Wolf Tribe.

By Jen McCarty

DEDICATION

This book is dedicated to Santos Bonacci, the great wonderful teacher of Syncretism.

PUBLISHED BY:

Blue Flame 5D Media

By Jen McCarty

ACKNOWLEDGEMENTS

I would like to thank the spirit of the land of India for impressing upon me the importance of working with an activated Altar and I would like to acknowledge my soul sister Zoe for helping me get this book in all of your hands - for doing the back pages, all the content and the formatting of the book.

TABLE OF CONTENTS

INTRODUCTION

This book has been a long time coming, so to offer some context as to why I am writing this book, I would like to share a story with you.

Eighteen months ago, I lost a Beloved soulmate of mine.

His death was untimely and a shock to everyone that knew him and loved him. Nothing could have prepared me for the journey of losing such a close Beloved or prepared me for the implications and ramifications that this has activated for me on my spiritual path.

When this occurred, I experienced the shutting down of many of my spiritual practices, as this experience shocked me to my core and put me very deeply into hermit mode, as a way of coping with the shock.

Before me losing my Beloved, I worked with an activated Fire Altar, cleaning it, tending to it, polishing my Deities, singing Mantras/Bhajans, and making daily offerings to my Altar.

However, when I lost my Beloved, the shock and trauma of losing such a close soulmate activated a profound shutting down of all of my external spiritual practices.

This put me very deeply into hermit mode, and during that grieving time, I focused solely on my internal Altar and my internal meditation practices.

I moved into a new property, and the landlady told me that she wasn't sure whether the fireplace worked. And in that 18-month deep grief period, I did not even attempt to see if the fireplace worked because I wasn't ready to sit by the fire.

I was in the Dark Night of My Soul, and I was embroiled in my internal process, and it was not appropriate for me to sit with the light of the Fire element at that time as I was assimilating and coming to terms with the extraordinary loss that my soul was experiencing.

Eighteen months after losing my Beloved, I had a very significant breakthrough, and I had a number of dreams which showed me that I was moving through a very dark, sticky layer of grief and I was coming to a place of assimilation and integration with the new state of affairs that my life was in without my Beloved.

One day I had this very clear thought to see if the fireplace worked, so I went downstairs, and I lit a piece of newspaper, and lo and behold, the chimney was unblocked. The fireplace was working.

I had been living in my new property for eighteen months with a working fireplace, which I simply did not sit with because I wasn't ready to go into the next stage of my grief process, which was truly the integration aspect.

On this day, I lit a fire and realised that I had experienced a profound transformation in my grief, and I experienced a very deep influx of spiritual light into my consciousness. This light brought with it a freshness and purity that I had not experienced in many, many months, and I looked around at my Altar, and I could see that it was very dusty.

The Untended Altar

All of my crystals had not been washed or bathed in salt water for quite some time, and there was a lot of stagnant energy that was stuck in my Altar.

When this brand-new influx of energy entered my consciousness, I was immediately guided to begin tending and activating my external Altar again, so I cleaned the fire pit.

I placed all of my beautiful, exquisite, powerful crystals in a salt water bath, I dusted all my Deities and feathers and all my spiritual objects, and I placed them back on my Altar, and I lit the most glorious fire.

I sat in my temple space in my home looking around, and I realised that in my eighteen months of inertia and grief, I had neglected to tend to the spiritual objects in my home, and they were just placed willy-nilly, wherever they landed at the moment that I moved into the property.

I looked around my sacred space, and I realised my whole entire temple space had not been tended to due to my entering into a very deep hermit phase of my life.

I immediately set to the task of cleaning every minute aspect of my temple space and my Altar.

I remembered implicitly the power of geomancy and how geomancy is connected to where we place spiritual objects in our home and how we use spiritual objects to enhance our manifestational powers.

By Jen McCarty

The Untended Altar

I immediately began the process of tending to my spiritual Altar in a way that it had never been tended to before.

The experience of cleaning and cleansing my Altar felt like I was dusting off the cobwebs of my tired and weary, grief-ridden heart, and I was placing myself back in the game of life, playing with a full set of cards, and playing my hands in an optimum way again.

As I was cleansing my Altar and internally cleansing and dusting off the cobwebs from my soul, I realised deeply and implicitly the implications it has for us when we do not tend to our Altar and how each speck of dust on our Altar space is symbolic of the dust in our own consciousness, which is symbolised by trauma-based thought forms, unprocessed grief and a lack of understanding of how our external environment is deeply connected up to our internal environment.

The day I lit my fire and cleansed my Altar was the beginning of a new cycle on my path, and I felt myself coming alive again. That whole experience has inspired me to write this book, because I'm sure many of you who are reading these words, who are not tending to your Altar, are unaware of the spiritual implications that this has on our soul and our psyche.

When we do not sit with our Altar, cleanse the objects on our Altar and make devotional offerings every day to our Altar, this has a detrimental effect on our spiritual health and well being, as we experience the accumulation of density, which serves to create a veil over the pristine glory of our true nature and the nature of reality.

By Jen McCarty

So I look forward to sharing with you all in these sacred pages ways to cleanse and tend our Altar, and I would love to share with you all some information about the history of Altars, why we have Altars, and how Altars have been used by many cultures on Earth.

However, I do feel it was necessary to start this sacred manual with this opening story, which provides a thorough and concise context as to why I have been guided to write this book at this time.

Chapter 1: What is an Altar?

Like all things in our world, particularly spiritual concepts, truths and realities all can be traced back to our Sun's cycle around the eclyptic wheel, and how the sun begins its cycle at the point of Aries, and moves through the constellations of Taurus, Gemini, Cancer, Leo, Virgo, Libra, all the way back around to Pisces again.

The Altar is connected to the astrological sign Taurus (all tau) and the word Taurus is also connected to the Torus field.

The Torus field is the symbol and actual patterning/blueprint of all Creation and is connected to the Atom and the patterning of the Atom.

Within a Torus field, you have a Proton and an Electron and an inertia Earth point.

The Altar holds a direct correlation to the Suns sojourn around the Ecliptic circle and its positioning itself within the astrological sign of Taurus.

When the Sun arrives in the position of Taurus, it is in a highly exalted place within the Ecliptic astrological wheel, and the word Altar is referencing this positioning.

All of our ancient cathedrals, temples, and sacred buildings are rooted in Sun worship, and most of these buildings are created with the astrological wheel at the forefront of their design.

Therefore, the Altar is positioned at the place of Taurus within most cathedrals and sacred spaces, and is symbolic of the exultation of the planet Venus and the soul's primary expression as a feminine Earth element. This is also connected to where taurus is allocated on the physical body, which is the cerebellum area of the brain and the neck, And it is this placing on the physical body which is overlaid onto the cathedral which gives us the area in the cathedral that is dedicated to the altar and is directly connected to the sign of Taurus.

The Altar symbolises the high and Holy place to which the soul sits in order to bask in its eternal and perpetual remembrance of the sacredness of all of Creation.

Altars are found in all societies and within sacred spaces; you will find universally that they will be placed at the top end of the building or sacred space, thus symbolising the Sun in its exalted position in the sign of Taurus.

The Altar is a physicalised expression of all that is Divine and is the Earthly actualisation of the spiritual realms as symbolised by the Sun sign Taurus, the second sign in the zodiacal wheel.

Altars are used as a focal point for spiritual service, spiritual devotion, and spiritual prayer.

An Altar is a spiritual tool that we use to connect with Source energy, aka Atum, which in ancient Egyptian is the word used to describe our Sun and specifically references that which cannot be divided.

That which The Creator sprung forth from.

That which created the primary duad of Creation.

The Creator and the Created.

The Altar is the physical space for the Created to revere and honour its Creator, thus always keeping our profound spiritual Source origins at the forefront of consciousness.

This is a subject matter which will be covered repetitively in the ensuing pages of this book, but I hope this is enough for you to be inspired to go and do some research into Etymology, the Taurus field, the true zodiac wheel and the primary duad of Creation, that being the Creator and the Created.

Chapter 2: The reasons why we use an Altar as part of our Spiritual Practice

In this next chapter, I would like to speak about the reasons why we use an Altar as part of our spiritual practice.

As I have touched upon in the last chapter, we use an Altar as part of our spiritual practice because an Altar is a physical and externalised aspect of the Altar of the Divine Being, which is the true Divine nature of God's Creation.

The Altar is also a symbol of the Cerebrum, the part of our brain that holds the Holy of Holies within it.

Each living Being is a temple of God. And within our own psychology and spiritual nature, we meet the High Priest and Priestess of our own internal essence, which is held within the Cerebrum and Claustrum of the brain.

The Altar, as mentioned before, is associated with the sign of Taurus and Taurus the Bull is connected to the consciousness that we have been created in God's image and thus contain and hold within our own consciousness the seat of the Holy of Holies, and the Altar is an outward manifestation of this internal place that resides within us.

And so therefore, the reason why we use an Altar is to point us directly to the truth of our Divine eternal nature and reminds us of who we are on a spiritual level. As it is within, so it is without.

The physical Altar is a mirror of the Altar within our own brain and consciousness. The reason why we work with an Altar is to create a focal point for our spiritual practice.

It is very important when we create an Altar that we maintain a connection with the five elements: Fire, Earth, Air, Water, and Ether. The five elements are the seat of all Creation, and this is symbolised again in the astrological wheel as the first sign Aries.

Aries is a symbol of the first spark of thought that separates itself from Source energy and says the words "I Am that I Am". Therefore, the Altar is a mirror of our Holiness and sacredness.

It is very pertinent that we make sure that we have all of the elements represented on our Altar because all of the elements of the Creator are Holy and are the elements that literally construct physical matter.

The Untended Altar

It is very important at this stage in our discussion that we all remember and hold at the forefront of our consciousness the fact that we exist in God's Creation and that God's Creation is Holy.

Every aspect of God's Creation is more Holy than we could possibly ever comprehend with our human mind. And the Altar is symbolic of this truth.

Chapter 3: Geomancy and the Altar

I would like to now devote this chapter to speaking about Geomancy.

Geomancy is, in fact, a Divinatory technique in its own right. The term was appropriated by 19th-century Western commentators in translated Chinese terms such as D-I-L-I and K-A-N-Y-U, which were then more commonly used in Feng Shui.

Whilst distinct techniques; Geomancy and Divination, may share a common historical origin; Feng Shui.

Geomancy, in this context, is referencing sacred objects and their positioning in our home, particularly in the temple space of our home and on the Altar.

A wonderful way to explain the power and potency of Geomancy is to use the example of a crystal grid.

Are you aware of what a crystal grid is?

A crystal grid is generally created on a sacred geometrical pattern, such as a circular board with a Flower of Life or a Shri Yantra symbol carved on it. This is the circular base for the crystal grid.

On the crystal grid, you intentionally place crystals and spiritual objects as a way to harness one's focus and intention on the manifestation of a particular area in one's life.

Therefore, Geomancy can be explained as placing particular objects in our sacred space in positionings that are going to enhance their magnetism and ensure our heartfelt Holy desire manifests into actuality.

For example, suppose you have on your Altar a statue of a Divine masculine and a statue of a Divine feminine, instead of having them on your Altar with many cluttered objects between them, such as un-cleansed crystals, wands, flutes, statues etc, it is important to understand that every single object that is placed between the masculine and feminine statues will act as interference on the pure actualisation of the manifestation, which is always to bring the masculine and feminine, the Electron and the Proton, into sacred union.

So, therefore, Geomancy refers to the positioning and places whereby we put all of our sacred objects on our Altar space.

It is very powerful when we use our sacred objects to create an etheric map of intention, and use our Altar space as a puzzle, so to speak, which shows clearly, through the use of potent spiritual symbols, the timeline that we wish to align with.

So therefore, it is very powerful on your sacred Altar to have a symbol of the Divine masculine and the Divine feminine with nothing in between them, remembering that any clutter or external energy that stands between them will interfere and encumber their union.

In my case, I have a candle that I light, and every morning when I wake up, I light the candle, which empowers and lights the flame of the connection between the masculine and feminine within me and outside of me.

We can do this with photographs, crystals, statues, tuning forks, and our candles.

Everything can be placed with profound intention so that we can use our sacred space as a map, which maps out in the unseen realms, the timeline which we want to experience in physical actuality.

Geomancy is a very powerful subject matter, especially in relation to maintaining our spiritual Altars. And a sign that you are not tending to your Altar is when you have just placed willy-nilly, sacred objects in positions next to each other that have absolutely no connection or may, in fact, cause an interference patterning.

It would serve us well at this moment to view the statues and crystals etc that we place on our Altar as the stars that make up a constellation. Everything in our night sky is intentional, and all of the angles and patternings are always intentional and working towards the manifestation of our Holy heart's desires. And it is the same with the Earthly objects we have on our Altar.

So my prayer is that you look at your sacred space and position everything in your sacred space in a way that reflects the flow of Divine energy towards the physical actualisation of your heart's desires.

For example, if you wish to manifest an abundance of money, a very powerful thing to do is get a newspaper and cut out a big wad of notes, and place them on your Altar. You can then have crystals pointing to that and even place this pile of notes in the centre of a crystal grid.

Everything is placed with the intention of a purpose, which is the actualisation of our deepest desires.

I hope these words have inspired you to look deeply into how you manage and maintain your sacred Altar space. And I pray that these words inspire you to work with the potent power of Geomancy.

I'd like to share a little anecdote that will illustrate this point. When I was living in Glastonbury, and I was calling in my Beloved, I had a symbol of the Divine masculine and the Divine feminine in my temple space close to my Altar.

One day I experienced a visitation by a real-life black raven who came into my home and was flying around. I asked the soul of the black raven what its message was for me, and the message I heard was, "He's coming home." I took that to mean that my Divine masculine was coming home to me.

This inspired me to go out and buy myself a black raven statue. I placed the black raven between the masculine and feminine statues in my Altar space and within seven days my Beloved knocked on my door.

The spirit of the raven was correct. The message was that he was coming home, and in fact, he did come home, and I am 99.9% positive that the reason why my Beloved showed up in this way was due to the positioning of the statues on my sacred Altar, and the subtleties of working with energy and intention, in terms of where we place and position the sacred statues in our Altar space.

This is an extraordinarily powerful practice, and prior to this moment, it has been kept within the highest echelons of the secret societies, but not any longer.

May we all understand the profound sacredness of all of Creation, particularly that which is natural, such as crystal, candles, fire, and all of the elements.

May we all remember to have a balance of all of the elements on our Altar and work with these elements in a profoundly enlightened, conscious, intentional, and sacred way.

Chapter 4: Cleaning our Altar and Altar Maintenance

It is very important that everyone understands that if you have an Altar, it is very important that you tend to it every day.

How do we tend to our Altar?

We introduce the elements of Earth, Fire, Water, Air and Ether into our sacred spiritual devotional practice, and we make sure that we clear away any dust and residues of old stagnant energy from our Altar every morning.

A wonderful practice that you could adopt could be going to your Altar first thing in the morning and cleaning it - working with the Earth element and cleaning away all the dust and residues.

You could then work with a spray, a vibrational essential oil spray, to spray your Altar and introduce the element of Water into the cleaning and maintenance practice.

You could then light a candle, light some Sage or Palo Santo or even light a Fire as a way to bring in the Fire element into your devotional practice and Altar maintenance.

You could also work with feathers to fan your Sage to introduce the element of Air into the Altar space.

You could have a picture of the Angelic realm, which would represent the Ether, and you could wave your smudging stick or incense over the picture of the Ether. Sound is also an extremely powerful and potent way to invoke the element of ether and is a wonderful way to cleanse your crystals and sacred objects.

It's very important that if we commit to the path of working with our Altar, we maintain our Altar and tend to it.

In India, every morning, most Hindu families make Puja with their Altar, and Puja consists of, again, working as closely as possible with the four elements.

Very often in Indian families, there will be an Altar space within the family home, often in the living room, and the mother or the father will make Puja every morning and light incense and wave the incense over and around all of the Deities that are placed on the sacred Altar space.

When we do not tend to our Altar, this enables the residue of stagnant energy to build up within our own psychic and spiritual field.

And as we tend to and cleanse our Altar, truly, we are replenishing and cleansing our own internal Altar, making sure that it is purified, cleansed, and free from negative, destructive thought forms and patterns. And so, as we clean our external Altar, we are 100% cleansing and purifying our internal Altar.

We do this to maintain an optimum spiritual alignment and vibration, remembering that when we do not tend to our Altar, this mirrors the stagnancy that we are most likely experiencing on an internal psycho-spiritual level.

There are many, many ways that we can tend to our Altar.

SACRED EXERCISE

Please use a sheet of paper and write out all of the inspirational ways you can think of to work with a very, very powerful and potent Altar space.

Chapter 5: How can having an Altar help us with our Devotional Practice?

There are many, many reasons how and why an Altar can help us with our spiritual practice.

The main reason is that the Altar creates a central focal point for us to sit and be with our Divine Selves.

We are Human Beings, not Human Doings, and so much of our Western society has indoctrinated everyone with a false notion of busyness, which is constantly taking us away from our Being-ness.

When we have an Altar, this is always standing in our home as an invitation for us to sit and be with ourselves.

In order for us to attain spiritual enlightenment, we have to find a spiritual practice that will enable us to become the observer of our monkey mind.

The Altar is a physical space that invites us to engage in this process of detaching our identity away from the temporary thought forms of the monkey mind.

Please refer to my previous books, where I share in great, great depth about the potency of working with a spiritual practice and why it is so important for us on the spiritual path to commit to a spiritual practice.

The Untended Altar

It is very, very difficult for us to attain the liberation of our consciousness without committing to a spiritual practice, and the Altar is the physical reminder that enables us to remember not to be identified with our thoughts.

When we have an Altar, this also works as a magical Geomancy tool whereby we can place certain objects in certain positionings that will profoundly enhance our ability to manifest proficiently.

Having an Altar reminds us of the non-secular nature of reality - that we all derive from Source energy, and Source energy is prime Creator - that which cannot be divided, also known in ancient Egyptian as Atum.

The Altar is symbolic of what is expressed in the Kabbalistic Tree of Life as the Crown.

The Crown in the Tree of Life represents the seat of non-duality and Source Creator.

And from Source Creator, the two polarities of magnetism and electricity burst forth.

Therefore, the Altar ever points us to the abiding memory of our eternal and perpetual Divinity and the place from whence our soul was created, aka pure Source energy.

When we have an Altar in our home, it serves as an anchor point for the Divine rays to be focused.

This creates an auspicious portal in our home for the sacred energies to flow unencumbered, particularly

By Jen McCarty

when the Altar is tended to, cleansed, and activated on a daily level.

I would like to create now a bullet list of all the reasons why it is very powerful and potent to have an Altar in our home;

- It creates a focal point for spiritual energy.
- The placing of the objects helps us align and manifest our Holy heart's desires.
- The Altar constantly reminds us of Source energy and where our souls originate from, which is Atum, the realm of non-duality.
- An Altar enables us to keep our thought forms cleansed and free from dross and low vibrations. As we cleanse each object on our Altar, we are cleansing the thought forms in our minds and polishing them so that they may return back to their pristine glory.
- It is very auspicious to have an Altar in the home, this activates a field of profound spiritual protection for all the inhabitants of the home.
- The Altar represents the high Altar in the church and cathedral, which is symbolised by the sign of Taurus. And this points us unequivocally to the reminder that we are all children of the Sun, that the Sun is the Source of life, and that we must keep God, Prime Creator, at the forefront of our consciousness.

Chapter 6: How can we connect our heart with our Altar?

In this chapter, I would like to speak about how we can connect our heart with our Altar and how we can connect on a deep spiritual level with our Altar.

The first thing that I would like to discuss is the fact that maintaining and cleaning the Altar every day is the number one way that we can connect with it.

Understanding that the outer Altar is symbolic of the inner Altar, and so as we tend to our outer Altar, we are truly tending to the Altar of our own Divine consciousness.

As we polish the statues on our Altar, we are polishing the auras of the Deities that reside within our own Divine consciousness.

This is the first fundamental step to connecting with our Altar, and that is, understanding that it is a living, breathing entity, and it is, in fact, a spiritual portal that you have created within your home, which must not be neglected, which must be tended to and cleansed on a daily basis.

This is the first primary way that we connect with the Altar, through the remembrance that it must be cleaned and maintained on a daily basis.

The second way that we connect with our Altar is to connect with our own hearts consciousness and remember that our vessel is the temple of God.

When you understand that you were created in the image and likeness of your Creator, then it will be easy for you to sit in reverence to the Altar within you and the Altar outside of you.

And so a fundamental way to connect with the Altar is to go on a journey to understand the true nature of reality and understand that we are all fragments of Source energy that burst forth from Source Creator into our individualised aspects, and we are all residing in these individualised aspects as we journey back home to Source-Creator energy.

When we truly, truly understand and awaken to our deep Divinity, then when we sit with the Altar and tend to the Altar, we are profoundly enhancing our connection to the spiritual realms and our connection to our own abiding, enlightened nature.

Another way to connect deeply with the Altar is through the practice of working with all of the elements, as I've discussed in all of the previous chapters: each day; working with Fire, Earth, Air, Water and Ether, and bringing those energies into our devotional time with our Altar is an optimal way for us to work with the Altar.

We do that by spraying Holy Water over our sacred objects. We do that by lighting incense or Sage or lighting candles.

We do that by working with Holy, sacred feathers and understanding that they have a connection to the Air element.

We understand that the elements are the primary way that matter came into being.

First, there was the Fire element, which sparks off in the sign of Aries. The next is the Earth element, as symbolised by Taurus. The next is the Air element, as symbolised by Gemini. The next is the Water element, symbolised by Cancer. And as we understand, the Ether is the mother of all of the elements.

So the way to work on an optimum level with the Altar is to find practices connected to our ancestors and understand how they worked with the Altar.

For example, in Hinduism, as I discussed earlier, each morning, the head of the house will cleanse the Altar, light incense and chant some Mantras.

Mantra is a very, very powerful way to connect with the Altar, singing songs about the elements or repeating the Holy names of God. These are exceptionally powerful ways to activate the Holy, Divine, sacred Altar.

Why is chanting so powerful? Because chanting allows us to connect with the vibration or emanations of the Godhead, and we become one with those emanations as we chant them.

The chants, such as "Om", are deeply embedded within our consciousness, and we all hold memories of chanting "Om". And so whenever we chant, "Om", we are connecting with our multi-dimensional nature and remembering our positioning on a spiritual level with all that is.

Chapter 7: How does one go about creating a sacred space?

The first thing that we need to do is decide on the area of our home where we will create our Altar. Will it be in your bedroom, your kitchen, or your living room? Or do you have a designated meditation space/temple space in your home?

I always recommend creating your Altar around your fireplace. Because when we light a fire, we are truly and absolutely invoking the most extraordinary spiritual energies.

How and why should I pray with my Altar?

We pray with our Altar with sacred intention and reverence for all that is Divine and sacred in this beautiful, exquisite world, the world that has been born of the energy of our Source Creator. We pray with our Altar, as a child would.

So much of the spiritual path is connected to us returning back to our original innocence, our true childlike nature. And having an Altar is an explicit invitation for us to return back to the consciousness of the eternal child that we are, that exists within the triad of God's consciousness that we have all sparked from.

The triad is the mother, father and Divine child. Therefore, to approach the Altar in the spirit of the child, we must put our ego aside and all addictions to our identity and the suffering that is ensued when we believe that we are this name.

Your true name is "I Am".

And when you sit with your Altar, it would serve you to let go of your Earthly identity and your name and bask in the eternal frequencies of your Divine nature.

As I have expressed in many of the other chapters, we work with the Altar by honouring the elements, particularly the Earth element, through the placing of sacred Earthly objects such as plants, flowers, leaves, rocks, and stones, and we keep these objects clean and tended to in our sacred space.

We have an Altar as a reminder for us every day to check in with ourselves on a spiritual level, to put aside the yearnings of the monkey mind to bask in the actualised frequencies of soul remembrance.

The Altar is a physical expression of our sacred nature and reminds us to stop, sit and be.

Whenever we bring our Divine Beingness to our sacred space, we fill our empty cup up from deep within by connecting with the Magnetic, Proton-esque energy within our soul psychology that enables us to connect back with the river of all Creation, the place from which all souls were born and burst forth.

So we work with the Altar in reverence of our true nature; that is God. God is not an ambiguous figure that sits on top of the cloud judging his children.

God is every single thing in nature. God is the trees, the leaves, the roots, the sky, the flowers, the animals, the crystals, the rocks, the oxygen, the birds, Human Beings, and children.

God is in Everyone and Everything.

And when we have an Altar, this takes us out of the nightmare of secularism and places our consciousness back directly in the heart of Divinity.

There are so many reasons why it is so extraordinarily beneficial to work with the Altar, one of them being when we work with an Altar, this turbo-boosts our spiritual intentions.

Working with the Altar is also very powerful if we wish to manifest something.

We can use the sacred objects in our Altar space and position them in such a way as to be a direct vibrational reflection of that which we wish to manifest. We can manifest money, abundance, Divine love, a particular job, and success, all through Geomancy and the placing of certain objects in certain positions in our Altar space.

When we have an Altar, we are keeping our spiritual house in check, and we are fanning the flame of our perpetual Divinity, remembering that we are all Source Beings, and we all spring forth from Source energy and are actualised as individualised sparks of Source energy.

We are all here to attain and bask in the glorious, saturated remembrance that we are Source Beings and each incarnation that we experience is an opportunity for us to deeply transform our consciousness and align it back with the pure Source Being that we are.

Our Altar helps us on every conceivable level to maintain our spiritual well-being and keep us deeply connected to our spiritual evolutionary path.

Chapter 8: How can working with an Altar assist me when I am out of balance?

Reading the previous chapters in this book, you would conclude that maintaining and tending to your Altar regularly is a way to keep you in a constant state of spiritual and vibrational alignment.

However, if you find yourself slipping out of your alignment - even whilst having an Altar, then I would like to share with you some of the following ways that your Altar space can deeply assist you.

FIRE

Let us start with the physical action of lighting a candle. When we light a candle, we are symbolising the flame of God that resides in the realm of non-duality, that which is known as Atum, the Fire Energy, which derives from Our Lord, The Sun.

Whenever we invoke the spirit of Fire, it automatically reminds us of our eternal nature, and the act of candle gazing is one of the highest spiritual practices that will take you out of the monkey mind and anchor you back into your spiritual alignment and your spiritual center.

WATER

When we work with the element of Water, for example we use a vibrational spray to spray our Altar or Aura, which derives again from the word Torus - referencing the Torus field.

When we work with the Water element and cleanse our consciousness and aura, this deeply assists us in removing all stuck, stagnant and dross energy that may have accumulated in our energetic, psychic field.

ETHER

When we work with the energy of the Ether through having pictures of Deities and Angels and Holy figurines, the presence of these statues reminds us of our higher self, the part of our soul consciousness that is forever at one with the eternal Godhead.

We are reminded that we are brave souls that chose to individuate as Source Beings to go on this wonderful journey of expansion into greater levels of Source remembrance.

EARTH

When we polish our figurines, this reminds us symbolically to polish our own consciousness and the thought forms that reside within our own consciousness.

AIR

When we clean and dust our Altar, this reminds us to clean out thought forms that are no longer serving us. Thought forms such as fear; fear of rejection, fear of abandonment. Also thought forms such as self-hatred and self-loathing.

We can polish our thought forms by taking inventory through journaling all the hurtful and negative thought forms that are causing trouble in our consciousness.

For example, you could take out your journal and write out a list of your beliefs that are not in alignment with the truth of your spiritual nature, and then you could get another sheet of paper and write out the opposite thought form.

For example; if thought forms of fear of abandonment plague you, you could on another sheet of paper create the antidote to that, which is; I am always loved and embraced everywhere that I go.

When you write out your new affirmations, it is recommended that you work with them in a way that will truly enable your subconscious mind to be reprogrammed.

I will often advise clients I work with to sleep with their new beliefs/thought forms written on a piece of paper and sleep with them underneath their pillow. Working with the powerful intention of asking the subconscious mind to take on these thought forms as truth whilst they are sleeping.

Working with the Altar helps us on such a deep level if we have lost our spiritual center, as the whole entire space of the Altar reminds us of the Holy Altar space within us and that we are non-secular Beings.

We are non-dualistic Beings, and our Divine consciousness is forever at one with Atum, our central Sun, and there is an aspect of our consciousness that is always, always deeply wedded to Source energy.

When we sit by the Altar, we are unequivocally reminded of our inherent and perpetual Divinity, and just this simple act is enough to transform our spiritual wobble back to one of stability.

As I've spoken about in great depth in all my previous books, the way to truly transcend your spiritual wobble is to find the spiritual practice that is going to enable you to become the observer of your monkey mind.

The practice that I advocate is the practice of resting as awareness for short moments.

Whenever we rest as awareness for short moments, this sends a pulse message to our monkey mind that it is no longer in control, that the Divine higher mind is now in control.

Suppose you do not have a spiritual practice?

In that case, the monkey mind will run amok and will do everything in its power to bring us out of our exquisite alignment and memories of our eternal inherent and perpetual divinity.

The practice of chanting Mantras, is another very, very powerful way to bring us back into our alignment and out of the experience of wobbling because when we chant and invoke these sacred vibratory patterns through sound, we connect on a very, very deep level with the moment of Creation, and this enables us to remember from whence our soul has originated from.

All that brings us suffering in this world is forgetting our Divine spiritual nature.

What brings us healing in this world is when we remember that we are offspring, fractals of God Source energy, and we are all here on this wonderful journey back home to Source, whilst temporarily having an experience of duality.

Chapter 9: Sound tools and working with the Ether

In this chapter, I would like to speak about sound and how we can work with sound when tending to our sacred Altar.

You will be familiar with the words;

"In the beginning was the sound"

If you trace back all ancient texts, you will discover that sound is literally the vibrational energy that creates earthly matter.

This is deeply connected to the decoding of the word Astro-Logos i.e. Astro-Logical.

When we really decipher those words, we understand that the nature of reality is encoded within our astrological zodiac wheel and this is brought into being through the sacred sound - the word.

Consider the Creator God Krishna and the fact that he is always holding a flute, which is symbolic of him singing Creation into matter.

How exactly does this relate to tending our altar?

In this book, many times, I have spoken about the five elements, Earth, Air, Water, Fire and Ether.

We have spoken in fairly great depth about ways to honour each of the elements when tending to our Altar, but we haven't really talked about the Ether and how to connect with the etheric level, in terms of tending to our Altar.

I would like to suggest that it is sound that connects us with the etheric level, and therefore using sound tools such as bells, chimes, singing bowls, mantras, and sacred instruments and playing these sounds in our Altar space and into our Altar space, will definitely clear the energy on the etheric plane.

What does it mean when we say clear the energy on the etheric plane?

Because we have incarnated in vibrationally dense third-dimensional matter, this means we can experience the onslaught of nefarious afflictive thought forms that very often don't even come from us.

They come from the collective consciousness.

These thought forms can easily accumulate in our consciousness and act as blocks and densities. Therefore, when we work with sacred sound, this is a very powerful method to clear these blocks from our consciousness.

Another really powerful tool to use is clapping. The energy of clapping is very, very powerful and not to be misunderstood.

Clapping holds an extraordinarily potent ability to be able to clean and clear stagnant energy wherever it is that we clap our hands, and this has been known by our ancient ancestors for Aeons.

It is widely known that clapping our hands on our Altar space significantly moves and shifts any stagnant energy which may have accrued.

In the beginning was the Logos.

This is such a huge realisation, to understand that sound truly lies at the heart of the creation of the material world.

Have you ever wondered why our organs are referred to as organs?

Because this points directly to the fact that they are connected to a certain frequency, and if they go out of balance, we just need to implement the correct frequency, and the organ will come into balance.

We can apply this principle to all areas of our life.

If we are stuck in thought forms of depression or suicide or wanting to escape this realm, very often it's because our frequency has become stuck in a low-frequency bandwidth. So therefore, for us to shift our frequency, it is highly advisable to work with the potent, powerful tool that is sound.

Sound is a vast subject matter, and it is something that I will be exploring in greater depth as I continue my evolutionary journey. It is my understanding that I will bring through a whole entire book, explaining about the power and potency of sound and how it relates to our evolution and how it can support us in attaining spiritual mastery.

But for now, I would like to leave you with a tip.

I highly recommend that you have sound objects on your Altar such as tuning forks, chimes, or any of the tools I mentioned above. And if you do not have the budget to buy these spiritual tools, then you always have the ability to clap your hands.

I recommend a protocol of everyday tending to your Altar and lighting a candle or a fire to activate the Fire element.

Lighting Palo Santo and using a feather to smudge your deities, which incorporates the Earth and the Air element, as we direct the smoke from the Palo Santo or the Sage or the incense onto our crystals and deities.

We connect with the Water element through working with powerful sacred sprays or Holy Water, which we can keep on our Altar space, which we can even bless our third eye with, and we can work on the etheric level with sound through using any of the spiritual tools that I recommended earlier.

What creative ways can you think of to clear the energy on your Altar and to feed your Altar and enliven your Altar with fresh energy every single day?

Remember that our Altar is a portal in our home that serves as a gateway between the seen and the unseen realms; therefore, we must tend to our Altar to keep the gateway from accumulating old stagnant energy.

By Jen McCarty

The Untended Altar

Sound is one of the most powerful tools that we have to keep our energetic space clear on an internal and external level.

As a Spiritual Teacher, I very often share light language in my sacred ceremonies. Light language is an anomaly for many people, and many souls have not remembered exactly what light language is.

As a person who speaks fluent light language, I would like to just devote a few words or paragraphs to share what light language is.

Light language is the language which comes from the guttural part of our soul. Most language has been structured in a left-brain fashion in many ways, and it is very logical and holds a linear patterning.

However, when we speak light language, we are tapping into the arch of the brain whereby the left and the right brain hemispheres meet and merge in the Centre. This produces sounds and codes and frequencies that are not linear words, but are purely coming from our soul consciousness.

As a person who has spoken a lot of light language and has listened to a lot of light language from other people, I would definitely say that it has a huge effect on the receiver, the intention that you have as a person that is giving the light language.

Many people use light language and are not coming from their heart space. They are almost using it in a militant way, and this can be extremely jarring.

By Jen McCarty

When a person is truly aligned with their heart and soul consciousness and they speak light language, you will feel butterflies, fairies and crystalline water sprinkling your consciousness, cleansing all of the density from your heart and soul as you allow yourself to bask in the sacred remembrance that the light language is invoking.

It is very powerful to speak light language in the sacred portal that is your Altar space.

Whenever we bring light language into our Altar space, we intensify the vortex energies of the Altar and call in more benevolent souls, spirits, Angelics Faes, and elemental beings to come and fill up our sacred home space.

I hope this chapter has been insightful and exciting for you and has set you on a path to deepen and develop your practices with your Altar.

By Jen McCarty

Chapter 10: How and why should I pray with my Altar?

This is a very good question and a subject that we can dive deeply into.

The way that we pray with the Altar is that we understand that the Altar is a living extension of our own psyche, our own soul consciousness, and so we must cleanse and tend our Altar. That is the first step with how we approach our Altar.

When it comes to other ways to be with the Altar, the following methods are what I would recommend.

The first method would be just simply to sit and meditate: find a meditative practice such as Vipassana or Transcendental Meditation, or just simply observing the in and out breath as the air goes through your nostrils. Also, candle gazing is very powerful. To sit and be with your breath, not getting lost in the rise and fall of the monkey mind. This is an extraordinarily powerful way to work with the Altar, and is definitely step one.

Every day I tend to my Altar. I cleanse my Altar, I clean my Altar, and I sit and I meditate. You can decide on the amount of time that it feels appropriate for you to meditate. I recommend starting with five minutes meditation and building up to twenty minutes every day.

The second way that we can work with the Altar is through working with sacred sound. You could purchase some tuning forks or singing bowls, and you could just sit and play the spiritual tools and allow yourself to bask in the resonance and frequencies that the tones emanate. This is very, very healing when we do this, and it is highly recommended as a way to get you into the meditative zone.

Another way to work with your Altar is to chant sacred Mantras. I often chant to Krishna and Radahrani and Rama and Sita. I find that when I chant, this takes me out of my monkey mind and it brings me straight back into my heart.

Another way to work with the Altar is by sitting at the Altar and pulling Angel cards or Tarot cards or any Oracle cards, dropping into your heart space and asking your higher self to give you clarity through working with the cards. This is a wonderful way for us to work with the Altar.

Another way to work with the Altar is to sit with your Altar and just simply be creative. Play musical instruments or just write or simply paint or draw. Being in your sacred space will definitely enhance your creativity.

When we create an Altar, this essentially opens up a spiritual light portal within our home, and each day as we tend to our Altar, we are increasing the velocity and capacity of our portal, enabling it to hold a greater level of spiritual light. So, therefore, whenever we are guided, it is always beneficial to sit by the Altar and just simply be.

The reason why it is beneficial to sit by your Altar is because your Altar is like a vortex. It is a place within your home where the spiritual connection to the higher dimensional realms is much thinner, and so therefore your connection with spirit will be exponentially enhanced every time you sit and meditate and pray with your Altar.

What is the difference between Meditation and Prayer?

Meditation is when we have a practice that enables us to not be drawn into the ups and downs and ins and outs of every single thought form that comes into our consciousness. Meditation enables us to become the observer of the monkey mind. Meditation enables us to sit with the silence of our being and to build up the muscle of emptiness, which is an essential part of attaining spiritual mastery. Please see my previous books where I speak in great depth about the importance of cultivating emptiness on the spiritual path.

Prayer refers to getting into a space of overwhelming gratitude and satiety for all the blessings that our Creator has endowed upon you and that are available to you through your imaginal faculties and your vibrational frequency.

The true way to pray is to say thank you for that which you are praying for prior to its Earthly arrival.

The Untended Altar

I am reminded of a wonderful anecdote which I shared in another book, but it's also appropriate for me to share it here.

There was a place in South America which was experiencing an extraordinary drought. All of the crops were dying and the villagers had an emergency meeting in the center of the town square. They all decided that they would all come to the town square on Sunday and pray to God for the rain.

When Sunday came, all of the villagers were on their hands and knees begging God to send the rain, and one little boy showed up with an umbrella. He came into the circle and he put his umbrella up, and of course the heavens opened and the rain poured down.

This anecdote is probably one of the most extraordinary ways to explain the power and potency of true prayer. Everything that our heart desires is already available for us in the spiritual realms. We just have to become a vibrational match to experience it.

This means that we have to build up our faith to believe that it is already ours.

When we can shift our own internal vibration, we enter into the frequency gateway of the manifestation of our heart's desires, and then it has no choice but to actualise into the physical realm.

Please see my book, "Divine Actor - I Am" and "Manifestation Mastery" where I speak in great depth about the power and potency of prayer.

By Jen McCarty

So therefore, the Altar is a beautiful hub within our home that reminds us of our spiritual nature and encourages us to work on the higher dimensional realms with our higher self to actualise the Holy desires of our heart.

It is recommended to work with an Altar to create this spiritual vortex within the home that will constantly and perpetually remind you of your Divinity and your true nature as God's daughter, God's son, as a fractal of Source energy herself.

Chapter 11: How can I use special Astrological dates to work with my Altar?

I have been doing a lot of research recently, and I have learned a great deal about Astro-Theology from the incredible author Thomas Burgoyne. In his great book, "The Light of Egypt", he explains the significance of the astrological cycle and how this relates to all Ancient Theology.

In fact, the entire basis of Christianity is founded upon the Sun's cycle around the astrological wheel. For example, the Sun dies on the cross during each of the 4 cardinal points Aries, Libra, Cancer, and Capricorn, and is resurrected again on each of these points.

Each of the astrological signs depicts a fractal of the soul's journey from its original split from prime Creator.

The prime duad, which was created in that original split, was the Creator and the Created.

In the infinite ovoid of white light that is Source, existing in and of itself, the first motion of its expression was a spark of thought, which repeated the words, "I Am that I Am."

From this point, which symbolises the sign of Aries, the masculine electric Fire sign, we move into the Earthly feminine Waters of Taurus, where the spark of energy, the masculine twin, must seek out a physical vessel in order to begin its sojourn into the Earthly plane. And here we meet the energy of Taurus.

This represents the Twin Flames as depicted in the Kabbalistic Tree of Life, in the Tarot, and as symbolised in all ancient religions, particularly Christian science, where we have Mary Magdalene and Christ, Abraham and Sarah. And in Hinduism, where we have Krishna and Radharani, Sita, and Rama, to name but a few of the primary duad pairs that fractal off from Source energy to begin their evolutionary sojourn around the astrological wheel.

When we understand that astrology is the mother of all sciences and we understand that all of our modern temples were created to honour the cycles of the Sun as living Sundials, we observe that in the great temples of Egypt where there are huge statues of Sun Gods, we notice that the beard that is always depicted with the Sun God is a symbol of the Sun rays that the Sun exudes when it reaches the mid-morning sky.

This points to the fact that our Sun and its astrological sojourn around the Ecliptic wheel is the science of the nature of human consciousness and depicts the precise story of how we arrived and were conceived in the great mind of God.

When we understand the significance of the astrological wheel, particularly the quarter points of the Equinoxes in Aries and Libra and the Solstice points in Cancer and Capricorn, we will understand that on these dates, the veil is extremely thin between the higher dimensional realms and the Earthly realm.

Therefore, it is always extremely auspicious to make special offerings to our Altars on these days, to hold ceremonies, to light candles, to chant Mantras, to invoke spiritual energies, to set intentions, to clear blocks, to deeply work in a pronounced way with the spiritual energies and your spiritual intentions on these significant quarter days, which are represented by the cardinal signs.

Forty days after each of the cardinal signs, we have the midway point of the astrological wheel, and we experience the cycles or the dates; **Beltane** on the 1st of May, **Lammas** on the 1st of August, **Samhain** the 1st of November, and **Imbolc** on the 1st of February.

This is referenced in the Bible when many times we see references to the forty days. This is pointing to the fact that these are also highly auspicious midpoint days for us to work with the spiritual realms.

I would highly recommend that you mark out in your calendar these extremely powerful, important, and significant portal dates and make an effort to work with these energies.

IMBOLC

For example, on the 1st of February in the Northern Hemisphere, we experience Imbolc. This is connected to the Goddess Brigit, who is the Divine feminine Goddess of the sacred Isle of Britain. Brigit represents all of Imbolc's energies, which is the promise of spring. And in the Northern Hemisphere, we will see the white snowdrops appear at the time of Imbolc. This is a strong sign from God, our Creator, that new life is bubbling away under the surface.

BELTANE

The next 40-day festival that we will experience is Beltane on the 1st of May. This is a very, very powerful day of celebration of the Divine Union, of the masculine and feminine Twin Flames, and the maypole is planted into the Earth. The Maypole is the symbol of the phallus, and the Twin Flames bind their Divine Union around the maypole that is thrust into the vagina of mother Earth. And the Twin Flames seal their love around the maypole.

LAMMAS

Our next forty day midpoint is Lammas, which is a ceremony that is dedicated to the exaltation of the Sun God Leo, and the ensuing harvest that we are about to reap in the time of Virgo.

SAMHAIN

And the final forty day midpoint is Samhain, the day we often call Halloween. On this day, the veil is traditionally very, very thin and all around

> the world, people come together to honour their ancestors.
>
> In Mexico, there are many beautiful Day of the Dead ceremonies whereby the town villagers go out into the local parks and town squares, and they create Altars for their relatives that have passed over the Rainbow Bridge back to the spiritual core. They bring photographs of their relatives, light many candles, sit up all night singing prayers and holding a vigil and bringing offerings of fruit and sweets to the spirit of their loved ones.

As you can see by this extremely brief description, there are certain days within our astrological wheel which are extremely powerful and potent. And if we were to use the energy of these days to set intentions and focus our heart on the manifestation of our Holy intentions, we will find that we will receive a huge amount of support from the spiritual realms.

So therefore, it is my recommendation that you dive deep into the understanding of these spiritual high points that have been spoken about in this chapter. And this is also an invitation for you to explore Astro-Theology's work in great depth because it genuinely brings understanding to many aspects of our world.

Astro-Theology points specifically to the symbology which deciphers all of our fairytales, all of our myths, all of our nursery rhymes. When you understand the great astrological wheel, you will understand all of the beautiful exquisite Tartarian buildings and pyramids that have been built all around the world that were created as temples of Sun worship.

It is also highly recommended that you place on your Altar some symbol of a pyramid because a pyramid is an extraordinarily high frequency symbol to work with. And when you place any intention underneath a pyramid, it infuses the frequency of the point of singularity, the zero-point field, to marinate your intention and allow it to be actualized with as minimal interference as possible. I hope that this chapter has been insightful and inspirational for you.

Chapter 12: What is an Offering?

I would like to devote the next chapter to speaking about offerings.

What is an offering and how can we bring the concept of offerings when we tend to our Altars in our homes?

Recently I went on a wonderful herbal course and the facilitator invited us all to go and connect with a Hawthorn tree. We were invited to connect our consciousness with the Hawthorn tree and ask the tree some questions.

We asked the tree a number of questions, and the level of communication that my partner and I received from the Hawthorn tree was amazingly exquisite.

One of the questions that I asked the Hawthorn tree was, "What can I give to you?" The Hawthorn tree very clearly responded that it absolutely loves to receive offerings, innocent offerings from our heart.

The Hawthorn tree explained to me that all trees, plants and flowers are living entities, living Beings. When we bring an offering to a tree, the soul of that tree feels deeply seen and deeply heard and loved and cherished.

The Hawthorn tree told me that just like we love receiving gifts, so do aspects of nature love receiving gifts. When we offer a gift to a tree or another aspect of nature, we are transforming our secular worldview and catapulting ourselves out of this material world into the New Earth, and we reach a heightened awareness that we are in a full conscious relationship with all of nature, as nature is a fundamental aspect of God's being.

You can apply this to your Altar. Your Altar is a living vortex within your sacred space and the more we cleanse it, sit with it, meditate, and fill up our Altar with our sacred energy, the more alive and activated the Altar space becomes.

So therefore, we can bring offerings to our Altar or offerings to our ancestors whose pictures we have placed on our Altar.

The offerings that we can bring to the Altar can be pieces of fruit, flowers, rocks, even a strand of hair is a beautiful, exquisite offering to make to either a Being in nature or to our Altar.

We do this to symbolically offer a prayer of profound acknowledgement and gratitude for our Altar, for being the vortex in our home that is keeping the veil thin between the higher dimensional realms.

The Altar is a vortex in our home, which is anchoring God's spiritual light in our space. The Altar is a Holy portal which truly can heal us.

So therefore, it is a no brainer to give sacred offerings to your Altar. I highly recommend that you begin this practice.

The Untended Altar

Making offerings to your Altars, making offerings to your ancestors through your Altar and generally connecting with your Spiritual Guides, your Angels and all the Beings in the spiritual realms assigned to assist you. It is always appropriate to acknowledge them and make offerings to them.

Making offerings is where we are going in the New Earth, where we all awaken deeply to the abiding memory of our oneness with all of Creation, our eternal oneness with all of nature.

We are all awakening out of the nightmare of duality, separation and materialism, to the truth that we are all physical aspects of God's Being.

Every aspect of this world is Holy and deeply, deeply sacred.

One by one, we are awakening to this eternal truth, and as one of us remembers, the sweetness in the Sun and the Moon deepens and ripens, and this sweetness exudes its blessings upon all the children of the earth.

By Jen McCarty

Chapter 13: What objects is it advisable for us to place on our Altar and why?

As I have mentioned throughout this book, it is always very auspicious for us to connect with the five elements; Fire, Earth, Air, Water, and Ether, and make sure that our Altar has symbols that represent each of the elements.

This brings great power and potency to our Altar space, and deeply enables the enhanced spiritual frequencies to flow through the portal that is the Altar in your home.

If you have a fireplace, I highly recommend using the Fire as your central Altar space and making a Fire every day, giving thanks and exaltations of pure gratitude to prime source Creator for this auspicious experience of being incarnated in this vessel at this time.

I would highly recommend having Holy water or Holy spray on your Altar to bless the Water and introduce the element of Water into the sacred space so that it can enhance all your prayers and manifestation of your intentions.

I would highly recommend burning incense, Palo Santo or Sage as a way to invoke the Air element as these beautiful smells fill up the Air with primal magic and memories of ancient days gone past.

I highly recommend working with the Earth element of crystals and statues and having twigs or plants or flowers on your Altar.

On your Altar, I would highly recommend photographs of loved ones that may have passed over into spirit that you want to connect with and seek out their council.

I would have pictures of Gurus, Teachers, Spiritual Guides, Ascended Beings, Angels, the Sun, and the Moon. I would have crystals on my Altar, and make sure that I cleanse them regularly so that they do not accumulate stagnant energy and remain in their primal optimum state.

I would also have sound tools, such as singing bowls, and tuning forks, and I would use the Altar as a space to chant Mantras to invoke the spiritual energies through sacred prayer and chanting, which will enhance the vibration of the Altar space exponentially.

The reason why we use these sacred objects is that they are very pure and they are connected to nature, and they hold a spiritual vibration and resonance.

We in western societies have been spiritually abused by Secularism. Secularism is Anti-God, Anti-Holy, Anti-Divinity.

Secularism has had everyone believe that they are third-dimensional meat suits who simply exist in these bodies for seventy years maximum working in the pursuit of someone else's dream, a corporate entity's dream, and then when we die, that's it, where nothing could be further from the truth.

The insidious and horrifically dark programming of Secularism has infiltrated every single aspect of society and has entrained and programmed everyone to forget their spiritual core.

That is why we have an Altar.

That is why we place these natural sacred objects on the Altar as a reminder of who we are on a spiritual level, that we are source beings who have been brave enough to split from source energy into our individualised fractal forms in order to grow and experience knowledge and wisdom, which we take back to source energy, which ultimately will expand source energy.

Source energy is ever expanding itself and fractaling off and birthing itself, and we are all aspects of source energy that are seeking out ways to enhance source.

Therefore, having an Altar in your space keeps you firmly anchored in the knowing and remembrance of your Divinity and the fact that you are on a Divine evolutionary pathway and that every aspect of life on this earth is sacred.

Having an Altar is life changing for many people. Many people have shared with me that they have experienced huge shifts in their consciousness and have been much more magnetic to miracles and moments of great fortune through the simple act of implementing an Altar into their space and activating the Altar every day through working with the five elements.

It is my deepest prayer that this chapter has inspired you to upgrade your Altar and has inspired you to work with it in a profoundly intentional way every day.

Chapter 14: How to tend to the Altar within and without

We have covered this subject matter many times throughout this sacred manual, but I would like to now devote a chapter to speaking about how we can tend to our Altar.

Making sure that your Altar is cleaned and dusted and that your crystals have been washed and bathed is the first primary way to tend to your Altar.

The second primary way is to make sure that all of the elements are represented within your Altar space.

The third primary way is connected to your personal relationship that you have with your Altar.

Your Altar is a spiritual vortex in your home whose job it is to attract you every day so that you may sit and be with your Divine Self in stillness and silence.

Your Altar is a space for you to be with yourself without the noise of the monkey mind.

Your Altar is a space for you to come and meditate, therefore it is highly recommended to find a meditative practice to commit to, and use the sacred space that is your Altar as inspiration to practise this spiritual tool that will enable you to attain enlightenment.

There are many spiritual practices that are available to us. I would like to share with you some of the most powerful and potent spiritual practices that I have used, which have helped me stabilise in enlightened consciousness.

Please, know I speak about these in my other sacred books, but for those of you that haven't read my other sacred books, I will mention them here.

The first spiritual practice that I work with is the practice of Transcendental Meditation. I have received a Mantra from a Spiritual Teacher and every day, I work with my Transcendental Meditation Mantra. This is an initiation path, and if you would like to practise Transcendental Meditation, then I would recommend doing a quick search online to find your local Transcendental Meditation Teacher who will teach you how to meditate using this technique.

The second technique is Vipassana. I have been very blessed to do a ten day Vipassana course, and it was extraordinarily blissful. In Vipassana, we are taught a very basic principle of observing the in, and the out breath as the breath enters the nostril. I find this is an extraordinarily powerful way to meditate and get into a deep meditative zone.

The next practice that I would recommend is candle gazing. Candle gazing is an ancient spiritual practice. The candlelight is so mesmerising for our Pineal Gland that we cannot help but look at it.

The Untended Altar

When we work with a candle, this is an open-eye meditation, and you can just simply soften your eyes, sit and gaze at a candle or a fire flame, and whenever you find your mind wandering off, you can bring your mind back to observing the flame.

The candle flame is a symbol of the Sun and is a symbol of the Fire element which reminds us of our spiritual nature and the realm that resides beyond Earthly matter.

I would like to now share with you the spiritual practice that I have been working with since 2012. I learned this spiritual practice with an amazing organisation called Balance View in Arambol, Goa, in 2012.

This is a very old ancient Dzogchen spiritual practice, which has been practised by Tibetan Monks for thousands and thousands and thousands of years in the Himalayas.

The practice is to simply bring your attention to the present moment whenever you naturally remember to do so. I liken this to jumping off the thought train.

Every minute of the day thoughts come along on a train and generally if we do not have a spiritual practice, we just follow the thought along to wherever it's going, and then it fizzles out.

When we commit to this spiritual practice, we are encouraged to jump off the thought train every time we naturally remember to do so.

By Jen McCarty

When we do this, we are communicating to our egoic monkey mind that it is no longer running the show, it is no longer in the driving seat, and that our Divine will is now in the driving seat because our Divine will is instructing our mind to stop this train of thought.

I consider this to be the mother of all spiritual practices, and it is due to this spiritual practice I was able to stabilise in higher dimensional consciousness in 2013.

I highly recommend working with the amazing spiritual practice of Yoga, finding a wonderful teacher, and then dedicating to your own Yoga practice. Yoga enables us to connect with our body in an extremely blissful way and enables us to clear much trauma that we hold in our body.

Another spiritual tool that I recommend is becoming addicted to going on rampages of gratitude. Whenever we go on a rampage of gratitude, we are essentially communicating to our egoic mind that it is no longer in the driving seat, that we are directing our consciousness to be absorbed in thought forms of appreciation and gratitude.

When we commit to this spiritual practice, we essentially begin to attune our consciousness to the higher dimensional realms and we understand that we are all simply transmitters of energy.

We remember that there is a very strong benevolent force in Creation that is keeping the stars in their place and ensures the bird song is sung every morning.

We remember that this is an energetic frequency band that is always available to us, and when we become addicted to gratitude, we attune our consciousness to this frequency band, and it really doesn't take very long for us to become one with this higher dimensional frequency bandwidth.

All of nature is loving and benevolent, and so when we commit to aligning our consciousness with focusing on that which is benevolent, we are endowed with the most extraordinary blessings of more and more happiness, alignment, synchronicities, and fortuitous meetings in our life.

I have spent a lot of my life journaling, writing out my fears, writing out my worries, and offering them to the sacred Fire. I always highly recommend working with your sacred Altar in a way that you can use the energy of the Fire to burn off old thought forms, patterns, and programs that no longer serve you or that are complete for you on a spiritual level.

I would highly recommend taking out your journal and writing out a list of beliefs that you have held which are no longer true for you, and ripping up that piece of paper and offering it to the Fire.

Working with the sacred Fire deeply supports us in the purging of this old expired energy.

We can sit and work with the Altar in so many ways. We can use our Tarot cards, we can work with our Angel cards, and we can lay down in front of our Altar and receive a crystal healing.

The Untended Altar

We can work with our sound tools such as singing bowls, tuning forks, sacred musical instruments, chanting, singing, Oming, toning, working with the energy of frequencies and vibration.

Have you ever wondered why our organs, such as our liver, our hearts and kidney, are called organs? This is because they are calibrated to a certain vibrational frequency, and if we experience imbalance in our organs, the ancients knew that we just had to sound out a frequency, and that frequency would return our consciousness back to the zero-point field, enabling our organs to again harmonise with their original blueprint note.

This is a very, very deep subject matter which I will speak about in further depth in my upcoming books.

When you come to your Altar, come as a child, come with the vibration of innocence, put all of your sophisticated knowings to one side and simply sit and be with your empty Divine Self.

All instruments in nature are empty. A guitar is hollow, a flute is hollow. Have you ever wondered why that is?

The reason why this is so is because the instrument must be empty in order to receive the grace of the higher dimensional realms, the Christic spirit you could say.

And so instruments are our teacher; they point to the fact that we must also find ways to commit to being spiritually empty.

By Jen McCarty

All of the tools that I've shared in this chapter are ways to bring you to spiritual emptiness.

It is my deepest prayer that you understand that emptiness is the greatest gift that you can offer your higher self because your egoic mind does not really know how to get from A to B on a spiritual level, and so your egoic mind has to be put aside.

This is what is referred to when we speak about becoming empty, it means not being filled up with the clutter of the egoic monkey mind that is addicted to the notion of separation and victimhood.

We must find a way to put down these thought forms and become the observer of them so that we can remember that they are not part of us; they are just appearing in the vast consciousness of all that is.

Finding a spiritual practice to become empty is my highest recommendation for you to truly work with your Altar in an optimum way.

As you approach the Altar as the empty channel and the empty vessel that you are and you commit deeply to your spiritual practice working with your spiritual tools, you will find that very, very quickly the grace of your higher Christic Self will fill up your soul consciousness and you will begin to feel amazing and happy and aligned.

You will begin to experience greater fortune, greater synchronicity, greater meetings of destiny. All of this requires you to become empty, allowing the egoic monkey mind to step aside so that the grace of your Christic Self may take over the show.

Chapter 15: What happens to us when we neglect or ignore our Altar?

If we take our memory back to the opening pages of this book, we will remember that this is what happened to me after I lost a very, very significant soulmate of mine, whose birthday it happens to be today as I write these words.

This experience catalysed my soul to plunge into a phase of inertia so that I could process this traumatic incident.

When I neglected my Altar, I placed objects around my home without any spiritual alignment or intention, and I was not cleaning my Altar every day or making Puja with my Altar.

During that time, I barely even meditated. It was enough for me to get through the day without being upset.

Therefore I can speak from firsthand experience about the implications it has on our spiritual well-being when we neglect our Altar.

What I experienced was that all of the dust that accumulated on my Altar was dust which was accumulating within my own consciousness. Through the action of not sitting with my Altar and tending to it and cleaning it, I was not actively engaged in the internal process of cleaning my own upset thoughts and deep sadness about what had happened in my life.

I placed sacred objects with the most extraordinary blocks between them. For example, on my shelf, I had a Goddess statue and a statue of a God, and in the middle of the statue, there was a crystal which was given to me by a very, very horrible person when I was travelling in India.

He gave me this crystal as a way to apologise for his outrageous behaviour, and really, I should have just let go of this crystal. But I kept this crystal for over 20 years, and this crystal was placed between the statue of God and the Goddess.

When I had my reawakening, which inspired me to tend to my Altar again, I was flabbergasted that, in my unconscious state, I had let that crystal stand in between the most important figurines in my sacred space.

I immediately took that crystal off of my sacred space, and I took it to the ocean, and I threw it into the ocean in order to assist me in transmuting the energies that man represented, which were very, very dark and negative.

When we do not tend to our Altar, we can unconsciously place objects in a way that is not going to assist us or enhance our heart's desires and manifestations which we wish to actualise.

Therefore, the message of this chapter is to be consciously aware of all of the sacred objects in your space and make sure that they are positioned correctly and in an aligned fashion that will enable the energy to be a mirror of your own sacred intentions that you wish to manifest out of the unseen realm into the seen realm.

When we do not tend to our Altar, and we allow the dust and the ash and all of the clutter to fill up our Altar space, this is deeply symbolic of us allowing our own consciousness to stagnate and accumulate extra clutter, through thought forms, which quite simply, most likely do not even belong to you.

When we tend our Altar, we tend to our own consciousness. We are involved in the process of evolution and involution. We are here to acknowledge the inseparability of the internal and external reality; as it is above, so it is below. This is the primary axiom of Creator.

Therefore, when we tend to our external Altar, we tend to our internal Altar. When we tend to our internal Altar, we are always invariably inspired to sit with our external Altar and tend to it in a way that is going to enhance our spiritual alignment.

We tend to our Altar to maintain our spiritual health and well-being. We tend to our Altar to keep our connection to the spiritual realms very much alive and anchored.

We tend to our Altar in order to clear away all of the clutter and dross that can easily accumulate in our psyche and sacred space.

We tend to our Altar in order to maintain a high level of spiritual connection to Source energy.

By Jen McCarty

We work with the elements of nature in order to remind us of where our souls originate from.

Our souls were activated through the Aries spark, materialised through the Venusian Taurus energy. Our mind and intellect was stimulated through the sign of Gemini, and we were all born through the motherly oceanic Cancerian Waters.

Ether is the mother of the mother, so, therefore, when we tend to our Altar, we are reminded of the potency to connect with the elemental Kingdom and Queendom, and to understand that in days gone past, it was the elements that were revered and not Human Beings per se, such as Jesus, Abraham, Mary, etc.

Back in the days before the fall of humanity's consciousness, we understood implicitly that the Solar Logos was the lord of our realm, and so all of our Altars were created in dedication to the Solar Logos and the understanding of the triad aspect of the God Source, which is Dielectricity/ Electricity and divine Magnetism.

That which is created from Source energy can be fractalised and fractalised, and therefore, when we create an Altar, our consciousness steps into the spiral of sacred memories of our true Divine heritage and spiritual path that we are all on.

The Altar is an anchor point for all of us on our spiritual path to remind us of our connection to Source energy, that we are all Source Beings who have fractalled off in our individualised aspects in order to go forward into the great realm of matter, armed with love and wisdom that we may attract greater levels of awareness and understanding, which we ultimately will take back to Source energy because Source energy is always expanding.

May these words deeply recalibrate your heart, soul and consciousness to the importance of maintaining your spiritual Altar.

May you love it. May you tend to it. May you dress it in all of the garments that nature offers us.

May you light your candles. May you burn your Sage and Palo Santo.

May you honour the Deities in your sacred space. May you remember to bathe and polish and wash your crystals, and may you remember to sit and be and meditate with your Altar.

By Jen McCarty

Chapter 16: A Deep Meditation

In this chapter, I would like to guide you on a very beautiful and deep meditation to assist you in connecting with your internal Altar.

So may I invite you to, if it's convenient to play some gentle meditation music and please read the following words. One suggestion is you could record the words and play them back.

Please find yourself now in a very comfortable position, beginning to take some deep breaths…..

Breathing in through your Naval centre…..

As you breathe out, relaxing your shoulders and relaxing your jaw…..

Continuing to take deep, cleansing, oxygenating breaths…..

On the next out-breath, bring your awareness to all of the places that your body is in contact with the bed or the floor, or the chair…..

Bringing your awareness to the sensation that you are being held…..

There is a force of great love, of great benevolence that is guiding you and cherishing you and holding you on this great and beautiful journey in matter…..

The Untended Altar

Take a moment now to connect with your heart and trust in these words…..

Trust in your deep, intuitive, childlike knowing and remembrance that you are not alone in this beautiful world…..

You are surrounded by a whole host of Angels and Spirit Guides assigned to you to protect you, nourish you, and nurture you on this sojourn in the realms of matter…..

Giving yourself extraordinarily, profound permission to relax deeply into yourself…..

Taking five more deep, cleansing, oxygenating breaths, attuning to the knowing that you are always eternally supported…..

And after the five breaths, visualise yourself standing at the top of a golden staircase…..

You see before you 10 golden steps…..

And we are now going to walk down the staircase…..

10 …..

9…..

8 …..

7 …..

6 …..

By Jen McCarty

The Untended Altar

5 …..

4 …..

3 …..

2 …..

1 …..

You find yourself now at the bottom of the golden staircase and in front of you is a large red door…..

See yourself push open the large red door…..

And you now find yourself in a dark tunnel…..

As you move through this dark tunnel, you are aware that there are crystalline sparkles of light that are sparkling in the tunnel walls…..

And you can hear a sacred tone…..

And this tone draws you ever deeper into the depths of this cavernous space…..

You find yourself now in front of a very small brown door…..

You realise that you must get on your knees to push this door open, so you get on your knees, and you push open this doorway…..

As you open this door, you find yourself in your womb space, in your Sacral area…..

By Jen McCarty

The Untended Altar

And all around you are the most beautiful, luxurious cave-like ornaments, furnishings and cushions made of deep reds, ruby, pink and rose…..

You look around this beautiful space and realise that there is a huge Altar which stands at the head of the cave…..

And you take a moment just to observe the exquisite beauty of this womb-like space that you have entered…..

You notice all of the lighting, the exquisite soft lighting, the curtains, the drapes, the fabrics, and the cushions are seeped in profound luxury and heavenly qualities…..

At this point, your Altar begins to sparkle and sparks of light pour from your Altar space…..

And this brings your awareness to your Altar space…..

And you notice that there is a Being who is in your Altar space…..

And it is your Twin Soul…..

Your Twin Soul is the aspect of your Soul that was created with you at the moment of your Soul's expression and separation from Source energy…..

You are the Electro and Magnetic original duad, and your material forms have been dependent upon each other…..

By Jen McCarty

The Untended Altar

You may or may not know this Twin Soul, you may or may not yet have met your Twin Soul, but please know at this moment, your Twin Soul is on bended knees and is polishing the Deities and statues on your Altar…..

Your Twin Soul is tending to and removing all of the dust and all of the clutter…..

Polishing all of your crystals…..

And is working at a deep level to assist in the maintenance of your pristine Altar space that resides within your Holy womb…..

You notice that you are standing back watching this scene, and you notice that your Twin Soul is in his or her illuminated form…..

They are exuding the energies of the Sun, and their Halo is activated, as is their aura…..

Their aura is filled with bright yellow and white light…..

You notice now that your Twin Soul is aware of you, and they telepathically ask you to come forward…..

You gently move your body to stand next to them…..

You are guided to sit down, and when you sit down, you kneel down…..

When you kneel next to them, they naturally start bringing over their hand and placing it on your knee…..

Notice that you offer your hand to your Twin Soul, and the feeling of connection is sparked for both of you…..

By Jen McCarty

The Untended Altar

They begin to telepathically tell you that they have been tending to your internal Altar since the moment your soul split from Source energy and was brave enough to descend into Earthly matter…..

They let you know that they are always with you and have always been with you, and will always be with you and that you are not alone in this world, that your true Spiritual Counterpart is within you…..

They show you the depth of their tenderness, love, and care by polishing all of the sacred objects you hold in your Altar space…..

Allow your heart to be deeply touched by this sacred Divine Union…..

And allow your Heart Chakras to both exude a wave of green light and form a heart symbol in the very centre of your Altar space…..

Notice now that this green heart is getting more and more dense and thick, and it is becoming like a rope which is just hanging in the air…..

You notice that there are two brown ropes that hang off the tip of the heart symbol…..

And you and your Divine Counterpart now take hold of these brown ropes, and you pull the heart over you like a hula hoop, and you seal your Divine Union in this sacred hula hoop…..

By Jen McCarty

The Untended Altar

As this happens, you notice that all of the candles on your Altar all light up spontaneously.....

At this point, the most extraordinarily exquisite music begins to play from the heavenly spheres.....

And you and your Twin Flame stand up and begin to come towards each other and hold each other.....

You look at each other and you are internally both saying, "Thank you, thank you, thank you, thank you for being here. Thank you for keeping your promise.".....

At this moment, you hear a knock on the door and all of a sudden, you are blessed with the presence of Mary Magdalene and Yeshua - Lord Sananda.....

They have come from the higher dimensional realms to acknowledge your Divine, Sacred Union.....

You notice that they both have a rose.....

Mary Magdalene has a red rose, and Yeshua has a golden rose.....

Notice now that Yeshua comes forward and gives the golden rose to the Divine feminine.....

And Magdalene comes forward, and she gives the red rose to the Divine masculine.....

By Jen McCarty

The Untended Altar

Notice now that there is a vase in the centre of the Altar, and the two roses are placed in the centre of the Altar…..

As the roses are placed on the Altar, you notice that they become much larger, and all of a sudden, a Source of pure heavenly water begins to flow like a waterfall from the vase…..

This is channelled all around the Altar, and the whole entire Altar has been activated with the pure waters from the Divine motherly Cancerian realms…..

Notice now that your Altar is being cleansed, upgraded, transformed, and polished, so that you and your Twin Flame may come back to this Altar at any moment to remember your eternal connection…..

Yeshua comes forward, and he blesses you on your third eye…..

Magdalene comes forward, and she blesses you on your third eye by placing her palm just in front of your third eye…..

They do the same for your Twin Flame…..

And then they both bring their hands in prayer position and bow to you…..

And they telepathically say that their work with you is now complete…..

They turn around and leave the space, and you and your Twin Flame are dancing to the highest Holy Celestial music that you have both ever heard…..

By Jen McCarty

The Untended Altar

As you are spiralling and dancing, a vortex of light comes down from the higher dimensional realms.....

And you are both bathed in this extraordinarily beautiful light.....

As the light continues on its descent downwards from the heavens, your two energy bodies begin to merge now.....

And you notice that there are two spirals of light that are moving up and down the pillar of light.....

And you notice now that there is one spiral of light.....

Now visualise this pillar of light in your own spinal column and feel the meet and merge of your own Twin Flame in your heart centre.....

Take three deep breaths.....

And if it feels resonant for you, repeat the words;

"And so it is, and so it is, and so it is."

This meditation is now complete.

By Jen McCarty

Chapter 17: How to feed our Altar

The Altar could be viewed as a living, breathing entity within your home, a portal, so to speak.

If you were to approach your relationship with your Altar in this manner and see it as a living entity, then it would make sense that the living entity needs nurturing and tending and feeding on a daily basis.

So what exactly does it mean to feed our Altar?

Feeding our Altar can refer to all the aspects of Altar maintenance, from cleaning and polishing our Deities, dusting off all the ash from yesterday's fire, making sure we have fresh candles, and making sure we have spiritual tools that will represent all of the elements.

Once all those foundations have been laid, then the Altar truly does become a living being, a living entity in your home that requires your attention and nurturance and is worthy of being sustained.

So in what ways can we feed our Altar?

We feed our Altar by sitting by it every day and acknowledging it as a living entity within our home.

We feed it by literally bringing it fruit.

This is a very common practice in many Hindu cultures. I've spent a long time living in India and Bali, where they live their life as though every day is a ceremony, and every home in the country has an Altar. And every day in their homes, they have Altars that are dedicated to certain Hindu Deities. And they believe that those Deities have sent a fragment of their soul consciousness to be, live, and reside in their home. And so they feel that they are duty-bound to feed the spirit of this sacred and benevolent Angelic force that watches and guards over their home.

And so in these cultures, you will find that every day the mother of the house (or the head of the house) generally will, before breakfast, she will make sure that she gets up, she showers, she cleans off the Altar, and she will then give an offering to the Altar. This will consist of fruit or rice or flowers. It could even be sacred crystals and gems from the Earth.

This is called Puja. This is part of Puja, and this is the aspect of it that is making an offering.

And this is how we literally feed our Altar. Some of us in the West have adopted these practices and have dedicated our Altars to particular Deities.

This is a beautiful way to navigate your relationship with your Altar. In my case, the leading Beings and Deities that I have are Babaji Herakhan Baba, and I have statues of Yeshua and Magdalene. And I feel a very, very deep affinity and connection with these Deities. And I believe that by having their pictures and statues on my Altar, I am invoking and creating a direct bridge to their spiritual energy so that it has a focal point to pour through into my home and my sacred space.

So, therefore, I am learning more and more to regard my Altar as something which must be fed. And to me, this purely means acknowledging the spiritual entities and Deities that are working with me in a Divine and exquisite way to support my evolution in this lifetime.

What are some of other ways that we can feed our Altar?

We can look to the East and their spiritual practices of making sure that our body is cleansed before we even come to our Altar. And then the next stage would be cleaning our Altar. The next stage would be lighting the candles and activating the five elements within our Altar. And then the next stage would be making an offering to our Altar, saying thank you for all the benevolent spirits that are watching over us and protecting us and guiding us on our evolutionary journey in this lifetime.

What ways can you think of to feed your Altar?

You could write a love letter to your Altar.

You could make sure that you pick your Angel cards every day by your Altar and invoke the presence of the Angels.

There are many various ways that other cultures use to feed their Altar.

By Jen McCarty

The Untended Altar

I love to bring fresh flowers to my Altar, particularly roses. I love the Divine energy that roses exude, and I know that the Deities that I work with love our physical Earthly roses.

When you understand the true nature of reality and that we are all Source Beings, the site of a rose is quite something to behold. And all of these Deities and entities reside in the higher dimensional realms, are well aware of the fact that the roses exist in the higher dimensional realms.

By Jen McCarty

Chapter 18: Last Thoughts

In the last few weeks prior to writing this book, I have gone through an extraordinary spiritual upgrade and I have experienced the balancing out of my left and right brain hemispheres.

Since I experienced my abiding awakening in 2013, I was not able to consume any external information as I was deeply assimilating all of the Gnosis that access to the Akashic Records was flooding me with.

However, the moment I reached the nine-year anniversary of my Ascension, I experienced a profound transformation, and I activated a brand new level of working with Mudras, and the Mudras opened gateways within my consciousness.

I realised that it was time now for me to profoundly deepen and expand my scientific knowledge about Source energy and how the Astro-Physical world and Astro-Theological world aligns with my deep soul knowing about who we are as Source Beings.

And so, in that time, I deeply opened my heart to extraordinary teachers such as Santos Bonacci, Thomas Burgoyne, Jordan Maxwell, and many other phenomenal teachers that helped bring all the dots together about the true nature of reality.

Because of this experience, my consciousness went even lower and even deeper simultaneously as I was able to truly understand and grasp on an Astro-Theological level the deepest, mystical understanding of each of the star signs.

And I understood deeply and implicitly that the whole astrological wheel is a fractal which accurately depicts the true journey of the soul's birth from Anti-Matter into Matter.

So, because I am fresh in these enlightened energies, this has inspired me to share in this sacred book about my relationship with my Altar. I would like to share with you all some words that hopefully will trigger your own memories of who you are as a Source Being.

I remembered in a way that I had never understood intellectually before that we are all Source Beings.

And what does that mean?

It means that we all originate in Source energy, and it was decided by our Creator and us that we would split forth from Source energy as a fractal of Source energy to go into the realms of matter, in order to attain a vast amount of experience -to ultimately bring back to Source energy and thus enhance the awareness of Source energy.

When you understand this, you understand that every single one of your brothers and sisters are Source Beings at different levels of evolution.

There are some souls that are very, very young and have just sprung forth from the white ovoid light. There are some souls that were born from their parents that existed within the white ovoid light, and there are some souls that are very, very, ancient who decide to return to this Earthly plane.

It doesn't make anyone any better or any less, and there's no sense of superiority because we are all identically matched Source Beings. But the moment we fractal off, we begin an individualised journey as a Source Being so that we may bring back to Source energy all our Gnosis and knowledge to ultimately enhance it again.

Each soul is on a journey to return back to purer and purer levels of Source energy. And that is why we fractal off and have these human experiences and descend into the Earthly matter in order to attain the greatest level with the greatest opportunity to deeply, deeply assimilate the truth that we are Source Beings.

We are Beings that are made of pure love and light, and that is who we are, and that is who we always will be.

We are all here to remember this and the purpose of life is to awaken to the truth that you are a Source Being, and we are all Source Beings, and there is no separation.

We are all here to absolutely support each other into their highest purest actualisation into being the actualised Source Being that they are, because that is the nature of Source energy.

Source energy is like the Sun. It radiates, and it gives, and it exudes, and it wants everyone to be happy, everyone to celebrate, everyone to dance, everyone to be in ecstasy, everyone to know the truth of who they truly are.

So when you understand that you are a Source Being and the Solar Logos of our solar system is the Lord our son which is referred to in all of the sacred biblical texts.

When you understand this, that nature is our temple, nature is the Holy of Holies, and we are nature as per the understanding of the releasing of the Christic seed in the Sacrum Plexus each month when the Moon sojourns the sign your sun was in at the time of your birth. At this moment, the Christic seed is released within the Sacrum Plexus.

And if we aspire to the path of purity and commitment and devotion to our spiritual path, the seed will rise up through the chakras and merge with the Pituitary and Pineal Gland.

And what will be released is the sacred marriage of milk and honey the Christic oil, which is the key to your own salvation and liberation and is the absolute highest spiritual jackpot that you can ever receive and experience as a Source Being returned this lifetime.

So when you understand the true extraordinary divinity of life on Earth, of the fact that every aspect of matter is dripping in Holiness and God's grace and God's thumbprint, it would make absolutely perfect sense that you would have an Altar, a sacred place in your home that honours the Source of all life, of all of Creation, and that this knowing will inspire you to step out of the secular prison of forgetfulness.

The Untended Altar

We have now entered into Aquarius and the golden age is upon us. So maybe you will take great light, love and inspiration from these words as we hold the Sun in our hearts, remembering that we are all fragments of the Sun.

I Am that I Am.

I Am Atum.

I Am that which cannot be divided.

I Am that I Am.

By Jen McCarty

CONCLUSION

In conclusion, we have covered a lot in this book. And this book, in truth, has gone far deeper than what I originally expected and intended, but that is all good.

I hope and pray that these words and these codes in these sacred pages will be like the purest heavenly water dripping into your higher mind, watering the seeds of your own sacred remembrance and Gnosis of who you are as a Source Being, as an offspring of the one fractal, the one Source God also known as prime Creator, that which we all are, and that we have all originated from in our individualised fractalised aspects.

May you take great inspiration from these pages and from these words, and may you apply these teachings with great childlike enthusiasm to the delightful Creation of your own sacred Altar or indeed the upgrade of your current Altar.

May we all be inspired in our understanding on an ever deeper level, the power and potency of Geomancy, that this is a gift that has been given to us by our Creator, that we may work with the energies of the Earth so that they may be mirrored in the higher dimensional realms, thus creating a portal for their actualisation and manifestation.

May the words in this book remind you that you are not alone, that you are infinitely and intimately connected to all that is. There is no separation in this world, except the illusion of separation, which is part of the matrix duality system that we all agree to incarnate into for the entire purpose of soul growth and expansion and greater contribution to Source energy.

May you feel the love in my heart that I hold for you, my brother, and my sister. And may you feel the Angels walk by your side.

I hope that you share this book with those that you love, so that we can pass on these sacred codes and messages to other souls that will benefit from them.

In closing, I would like to remind you that your Being is so deeply valued and treasured in this world. Your being here means everything to all of us. We all celebrate you. We are all so grateful to you.

You are making God so happy now with your commitment to the right-hand path, the path of making choices that will assist you to preserve your life force energy, that will assist you to become ever more magnetic to your soul's Holiest and sacred desires.

May you bask now in the glorious remembrance of the truth of your eternal heritage.

You are eternally loved and your Creator ever watches over you in abiding commitment and eternal service to your nourishment and wellbeing.

This has been a wonderful and extraordinary journey to bring through these sacred words. I highly recommend reading all my other books. They are filled with extraordinary Gnosis presented in a very understandable and easily digestible manner.

I'm sure you will gain much spiritual expansion from the experience.

In Love and Eternal Light

Jen.

PLEASE LEAVE A REVIEW FOR

THE UNTENDED ALTAR

ON AMAZON

It is my deepest and sincere prayer that this book has given you a profound understanding of the Spiritual Altar both within and without, and I hope that you will find this book to be a valuable resource in your spiritual library.

If you have enjoyed this book and found it helpful, please consider leaving a review on Amazon. Your reviews are hugely helpful to me as a published author and will help others be able to find this book in the Amazon search results.

THE UNTENDED ALTAR - BOOK REVIEWS

"After reading these preview chapters I feel so humbled and privileged to be able to receive such incredibly deep and profound Divine knowledge of the highest calibre. In every sentence there is a gem, a beautiful pearl of wisdom, that I am stretching my consciousness to digest. The connections to the ancient understanding of Astrology, Tartarian secrets and the whole universe of magic and the manifestation of

your highest wishes waiting to be revealed to any person who has tended to their heart flame.

Synchronistically with the loss of her soulmate 18 months back and the heart crushing consequences, I went through a similar closing of my heart myself during the same period. I realise myself after reading these pages, the truth of how a closed off heart manifests like a dusty, cloudy layer around you, separating yourself from your true, pure spark.

In "The Untended Altar" - Jen describes when your heart closes itself to digest the deepest loss and pain, you often don't tend to your outer altar, a place in your home you intend to make sacred, you let it dust down, get cluttered, unintentional and dense. This directly correlates to your own inner connection to Source energy and feelings of being dead and disconnected.

As I read on I felt an activating spark of magic realising this is something I have never truly understood before. Jen is showing how your internal and external altars are directly connected and by tending daily to keep your external altar clean and uncluttered you can directly activate an energetic alignment of Life, Love and magic in your life." **Kristine S.**

"The Untended Altar" really hit home for me on so many levels - energetically, spiritually, physically, mentally and emotionally and is a reflection of our inner vibration & internal divinity.

The Untended Altar

While reading this book, I had a deep remembrance of all of my combined and simultaneous incarnations and her words brought me back to centre with my true divine soul essence & energetic blueprint.

This book illuminates intention and awareness on levels unprecedented. It allows you to get very clear about what you wish to bring through, manifest and what timeline you align with. It reflects the co-creative power and connection with you, your mission, the universe and Source." ***Whitney E.B.S.***

"The Untended Altar" has really lit a spark for me. I've used and created altars as part of my spiritual practice for many years. However, I haven't ever really engaged with them, or cleansed them once activated. This book was a real wakeup call to tap into the power of the altar and its energy by tending to it lovingly, just as carefully as I would what I'm looking to manifest. I'm off to clear the space now and consider the 5 elements, intention and add it to my daily spiritual practice. Thank you Jen for such a great book." ***Romella J.***

By Jen McCarty

OTHER BOOKS PUBLISHED

BY JEN MCCARTY

AVAILABLE ON AMAZON NOW!

Jen has published a number of books;

- **Twin Flames and The Event** – A Message for the 144,000 Lightworkers
- **No More Crumbs** – An Empowerment Manual for the Divine Feminine
- **Law of Attraction** – Little Instruction Book
- **Manifestation Mastery** – How to Work with the Quantum Field and Hack the Matrix
- **Divine Actor - I AM** - A book that has been created to take humanities consciousness to the next level
- **The Untended Altar** - How to work with the Spiritual Vortex in your home

TWIN FLAMES AND THE EVENT

A MESSAGE FOR THE 144,000 LIGHTWORKERS

- What is a Twin Flame?
- Does everyone have a Twin Flame?
- How do I meet my Twin Flame?
- Why are Twin Flames such a hot topic at the moment?
- And what do Twin Flames have to do with the Great Awakening that we are experiencing as a collective?

These are some of the questions that will be answered in this book!

Billions of books have been created in the world, and you were drawn to this book for a reason. Your higher self has brought you to this book, and this is because it contains codes that are specifically connected to you and your evolutionary journey towards spiritual mastery and eternal union with your Twin Flame.

By Jen McCarty

PRAISE FOR TWIN FLAMES AND THE EVENT

"After a lifelong struggle of working to overcome the effects of extreme abuse in my childhood, I have arrived at perhaps the most challenging period of my life, facing PTSD, flashback after flashback, and just so much pain. I write this now because I want to say that this book, TWIN FLAMES AND THE EVENT, has come to me in the midst of this processing. I didn't know if I could even concentrate on the book, each line, or each word. But guidance said, "Read, even just one sentence for now." So I did!

Over the past 20+ years of my spiritual journey, I have purchased countless good books, but I honestly feel that this one is superior to all of those. Jen McCarty has channelled a book like no other! Immense gratitude, Jen McCarty! This book will change countless lives! I know it's changing mine! Transformative, Beautiful, Relatable, Divine! What a gift!"
Jill

"Twin Flames and the event" is a rare gem of a book. Within minutes of reading I had received such great insight that I literally had to take time out to reassess my life. I was then able to reframe past life events in such a way that I felt enormous relief and a sense of peace as I realised that everything in my life had in fact played out to perfection.

After this realisation I was straight back into the book, for it is extremely compelling as there is a plethora of information. Jen McCarty writes as an authority on the subject of Twin Flames, which is a very hot topic at the moment. But Jen has been interested in this field since her awakening in 1995 but has waited until this time to put her knowledge into a book for the general public.

For it is now perfect timing: the book was released in the first season of Aquarius after the planet's shift into the age of Aquarius at the last equinox. It is then no surprise that this is no ordinary book, for it is infused with energetic codes to trigger remembrances and awakenings." ***Kate***

SCAN ME

https://qrco.de/bcFmjG

TWIN FLAMES AND THE EVENT on AMAZON

SCAN QR CODE ABOVE

By Jen McCarty

TWIN FLAMES AND THE EVENT WORKBOOK

AND MP3 ACTIVATIONS

Jen has written a workbook which is the perfect companion for the sacred text – Twin Flames And The Event.

Halfway through writing Twin Flames and The Event – I was very strongly guided by spirit to create a workbook that would accompany this powerful sacred scripture. So therefore, I followed this guidance and brought through an amazing offering that will assist you to deeply and understand and assimilate all of the information and codes that are shared in the book.

I would highly recommend everybody work with the workbook, as the exercises and MP3 activations work on a deeply subconscious level and work with the incredible power of symbols, which are **the** language of the unconscious mind.

If you really want to experience a shift in your vibrational reality and receive great assistance in truly becoming one with your higher self, then I highly recommend you gift yourself this beautiful workbook that goes alongside this sacred text.

By Jen McCarty

Working with the MP3 activations which accompany the workbook deeply and profoundly fast tracks your spiritual ascension path and enables you to activate these codes of transformation very swiftly and efficiently within your energetic system. I cannot recommend working with these activations' highly enough.

SCAN ME

https://qrco.de/bcfHWo

TWIN FLAMES AND THE EVENT WORKBOOK on AMAZON

SCAN QR CODE ABOVE

NO MORE CRUMBS

AN EMPOWERMENT MANUAL FOR THE DIVINE FEMININE

Women all around the world have been programmed to accept crumbs. This has to end. Women are goddesses and need to transform their inner world to fully and completely accept this truth. As soon as a woman accepts that she is a goddess she collapses all old patterns pertaining to accepting crumbs and she co-creates brand-new subconscious patterns which support her to attract devotion from her predestined true love.

The world is changing before our eyes and never before has it been so important for Twin Flame / God mates to come together.

This book will help you to so deeply and profoundly release all programming around accepting crumbs in romantic relationships. It will transform your inner beliefs and subconscious mind and assist you to attract your true love with ease and grace and great swiftness.

By Jen McCarty

PRAISE FOR NO MORE CRUMBS

"From the opening paragraph I felt held and lifted, an expansion of my heart and activity in my third eye. Part of me was shouting yes! I remember and the words flowed into my consciousness, being and belong there. As I read on, I recognised the truth of your words and the patterns of my relationships and here was guidance to co-create the reality of my desire. The wisdom shared illuminated a reinterpretation of events and a deeper understanding of who I, we are. This book is a compass for all feminines' to step into their power and navigate their lives. Thank you is insufficient for such an amazing gift of guidance." ***Namaste, Karen***

"I have read the first five chapters of your amazing book "No More Crumbs" and I was flabbergasted at how much this book resonated with my healing journey. After I had read the chapters I experienced many activations and synchronicities started to manifest in my life. I was able to capture all of the red flags I have overlooked due to the conditioning and programming. I immediately stopped tolerating standoffish behaviour from men. I started to manifest a new tribe of nice, fun and genuine people to hang out with. I even got two interviews for two jobs which I had recently applied for. I am so humbled at this opportunity you have given me, Jen. it will be an honour to buy and read the whole book and apply it to my life." ***Lisseth***

NO MORE CRUMBS

AN EMPOWERMENT MANUAL FOR THE DIVINE FEMININE

SCAN ME

https://qrco.de/bdZbpN

NO MORE CRUMBS on AMAZON

SCAN QR CODE ABOVE

NO MORE CRUMBS WORKBOOK AND MP3 ACTIVATIONS

Working with the MP3 activations which accompany the No More Crumbs Workbook deeply and profoundly fast tracks your spiritual ascension path and enables you to activate these codes of transformation very swiftly and efficiently within your energetic system. I cannot recommend working with these activations' highly enough.

By Jen McCarty

SCAN ME

https://qrco.de/bcgel1

NO MORE CRUMBS WORKBOOK on AMAZON

SCAN QR CODE ABOVE

LAW OF ATTRACTION

LITTLE INSTRUCTION BOOK

The book consists of an introduction whereby I share with you all my downloads about how to work very deeply and powerfully with the law of attraction and the rest of the book is a combination of quotes and affirmations from well-known people that have worked successfully with the law of attraction.

This is a book of miracles, a tale of timeless truth and a promise to the most ancient part of ourselves to remember and align with the highest vibration of who we are.

By Jen McCarty

PRAISE FOR LAW OF ATTRACTION LITTLE INSTRUCTION BOOK

"Absolutely awesome book just as you would expect from Jen. She really is a beautiful being of light with a heart that desires everyone else's light to shine. Thank you Jen." **Carla.**

SCAN ME

https://qrco.de/bcgeI1

LAW OF ATTRACTION - LITTLE INSTRUCTION BOOK on AMAZON

SCAN QR CODE ABOVE

MANIFESTATION MASTERY

HOW TO WORK WITH THE QUANTUM FIELD AND HACK THE MATRIX

This is not a normal book that you are holding in your hands. This is a Manifestation Mastery Manual.If you take heed to the guidance and protocols that are shared in this powerful manuscript, you will become a Master Manifestor.

When we focus simply on the Law of Attraction, we miss out on so many fundamental aspects of becoming a proficient Master Manifestor. The reason for this is that it does not talk about the Law of Attunement, the Law of Frequency and the Law of Choice.

In this book, you will receive a deep transmission into all the different aspects of Manifestation Mastery that "The Secret" did not cover. In this powerful and life-changing manual, I share many of the previously secret and hidden manifestation hacks that will enable you, the layperson, to become an extremely potent Master Manifestor.

After reading this book, you will never be the same again, as this book is infused with enlightenment codes

By Jen McCarty

that will enable you to awaken out of the long, drawn out collective spiritual slumber.

This book is a game changer.

This book will enable you to manifest the life of your dreams.

THis book will enable you to manifest the income of your dreams.

This book will teach you how to manifest the relationship of your dreams.

Nothing has been left out.

The most deepest, powerful, ancient Manifestation Mysteries for the first time have been openly shared.

PRAISE FOR MANIFESTATION MASTERY

"Another outstanding book from Jen McCarty who shares her divine knowledge, codes and blueprint for all you need in aligning with the quantum field. I literally had goosebumps even holding this book when it arrived and the incredible images and codes all delivered from Jen hold next level information which is being accessed as you read. I just keep rereading it all at the moment as I know the codes are going deeper each time and it is such a great book to have and hold

near you. Thanks as always Jen for your service to our healing and mastering the magnificence we all hold and can indeed embody." ***Ruby P.***

"I highly recommend this amazing book by Jen McCarty. It is a next level guide to manifestation. It is really beautiful with gorgeous pictures, quotes and invaluable teaching, guidance and exercises. A real life changing book. The light codes are amazing and I had several A-ha moments from doing the exercises. I could feel the energy in my body. Notably the crown chakra. A worthwhile investment." ***S.***

MANIFESTATION MASTERY

HOW TO WORK WITH THE QUANTUM FIELD AND HACK THE MATRIX

SCAN ME

https://qrco.de/bchMjW

MANIFESTATION MASTERY on AMAZON

SCAN QR CODE ABOVE

DIVINE ACTOR - I AM

A BOOK THAT HAS BEEN CREATED TO TAKE HUMANITIES CONSCIOUSNESS TO THE NEXT LEVEL

By Jen McCarty

This book explains in great depth the spiritual purpose behind acting and why acting is considered the highest spiritual art form. This book takes the whole sacred gift of acting and places it back in the spiritual heights where it truly belongs.

The message of this book is a profound invitation for us to once and for all mature as a human family. This is the most potent manifestation practice that has ever been shared to date on the earth plane in recent times.

May we all remember that the subconscious mind does not know the difference between something it sees with its physical eyes or what it imagines. The practice that is shared in this sacred book is one of the highest initiations in the spiritual mystery schools and has previously been entirely hidden and denied to humanity, until now.

Please understand that the words, messages and protocols in this sacred manual are compelling and life-changing, and you will experience the rapid manifestation of your heart's desires if you apply the teachings shared in this manual.

PRAISE FOR DIVINE ACTOR - I AM

"I love your books! Each book takes me on a deeper level of myself, this one is another amazing book. I see that I have work to do, which I am grateful for and blessed to be given the guidance." ***Kate.***

By Jen McCarty

"I consider this book to be a major catalyst in the process of awakening to our divine purpose and our divine role as we take each step forward to embody our chosen place within humanity. This text offers a re-orientation of our sacred responsibility as we walk this Earth plane. It is a literal re-membering of why we are here, and it affords us the tools to broaden each step. It truly is a gift." ***Kelly.***

SCAN ME

https://qrco.de/bdPJ1L

MANIFESTATION MASTERY on AMAZON

SCAN QR CODE ABOVE

AUDIOBOOKS

Please know that I have bought through the audio versions of my books.

It is very powerful to receive the audio version as there is an opportunity to receive my words and my voice. Our voice is a reflection of our soul signature and enables us to very deeply connect with the soul frequency of the person that is sharing.

AUDIOBOOKS REVIEWS

"There is something about Jen's voice and the messages that she brings forth that connects deeply with my inner knowing. I know I will listen back many, many, many times." ***Jade W.***

"So deeply profound and enlightening. This book has brought me to a wonderfully heightened state of awareness and has prompted me to want more from the author." ***A.***

SCAN ME

https://qrco.de/bcFn7f

AUDIOBOOKS AUDIBLE LINK

SCAN QR CODE ABOVE

By Jen McCarty

PLEASE LEAVE A REVIEW ON AUDIBLE

If you have enjoyed listening to any of my audiobooks, please consider leaving a review on Audible. Your reviews are hugely helpful to me as a published author and will help others be able to find my audiobooks in the Audible search results.

OVERVIEW OF JENS SACRED OFFERINGS

Jen is very excited to share the original and powerful modalities which her higher-self has shared with her. She is offering regular training throughout the year as well as many self-paced programs. These trainings and programs are packed with Ascension codes that will enable you to up level your spiritual vibration very quickly and very efficiently.

Jen is an extremely powerful facilitator, and it is highly recommended to sign up to the training whereby you get close access to Jen. If you are unable to attend the training, then we highly recommend working with the self-paced programs. Jen is continuously bringing through powerful life changing programs that will massively affect your spiritual vibration and enable you to stabilise in Unity Consciousness.

Here is an overview of Jens' Sacred Offerings;

- Monthly Global Transmissions
- 21 Day DNA Activation Programs
- Self-Paced Online Programs
- Books, Audiobooks, Workbooks
- MP3 Meditations
- Jens Album "Love Songs for God" will be released by Valentines Day 2023.

SCAN ME

https://qrco.de/bcFmd2

JENS SACRED OFFERINGS ON HER WEBSITE

SCAN QR CODE ABOVE

MONTHLY GLOBAL TRANSMISSIONS

Since 2016 Jen has been hosting regular global transmissions on numerological portal dates such as 2:2, 3:3, 4:4 etc. Also, on Pagan holidays such as Samhain Imbolc, Equinox and Solstice. The reason for this is that it is so important that the Awakened Star Crew gather together on powerful dates such as these, in order to align our will and intention, with the will and intention of Mother-Father God.

21 DAY DNA ACTIVATION PROGRAMS ONLINE PROGRAMS

Jen has produced a number of 21-day DNA activation programs on;

- Attract 1 Million Followers
- Miracle Hair Growth
- EMF Protection
- Abundance
- Age Regeneration
- Divine Love

Each 21 Day Program comes with a meditation which is highly activating for your DNA plus an E-Book with exercises to follow during the 21 days.

It is highly advisable to work with a program for 21 days as it gives you enough time to take on a brand-new habit and it is our habits that ultimately change our life. I have been getting the most phenomenal feedback from all the people in my community that have been doing these programs and they are highly advisable if you wish to fast-track your spiritual evolution.

MP3 MEDITATIONS

This is an extremely powerful MP3 MEDITATION series designed to fast track you towards full and triumphant Twin Flame union, there are codes and frequencies embedded into these meditations that work specifically to bring you fully home to yourself on a spiritual level, and return you to full physical union with your eternal beloved on all planes of consciousness.

These meditations attune you specifically to 5th dimensional consciousness, and the results so far have been truly mind blowing with many, many people reporting crying the deepest tears they have ever known, and many being miraculously contacted by their Twin Flame around the time of completing these activations.

SPECIAL MP3 MEDITATIONS

I also have two special activations; one is called the "Yoni Nidra" and the other is called "Miracle IBS Healing". These are long in-depth healing meditations that will massively affect your healing journey and spiritual vibration.

SELF-PACED ONLINE PROGRAMS

Jen will also be creating a number of self-paced online programs which are an opportunity to go on an extremely powerful, deep, and intimate journey with Jen to massively transform programming around wealth, love and belonging.

Please look out for all the information on Jen's powerful self-paced online programs soon to be launched on her website:

- Prosperity Unleashed
- Twin Flame
- Nervous System Recalibration
- Write and Publish your Book

SACRED MUSIC

Jens Album “Love Songs for God” will be released by Valentines Day 2023.

ABOUT THE AUTHOR - JEN MCCARTY

Widely known as the healer of healers - Jen McCarty has earned the most astonishing place in everyone's heart. As a published author - Jen assists people with addiction recovery, as well as helping many people heal their core wounds on a soul level. Jen had a massive life-changing Kundalini Awakening when she was just 21, in the Himalayas in Northern India, chanting the mantra "Om Namah Shivaya". From that moment on she passed over the threshold from third-dimensional consciousness to fully stabilising in fifth-dimensional consciousness.

Jen has since devoted her whole adult life serving her brothers and sisters and has been blessed with a massive amount of extremely dedicated followers over the last 5 years and has built up a social media following of over 175,000 people.

Jen specialises in working with the reunion of Twin Flames and the removal of roadblocks that stand in the way of that. She is an awakened Spiritual Teacher, deeply and highly skilled at facilitating a space for all those who she comes into contact with. She has a phenomenal track record in uniting many, many Twin Flames, assisting them to connect with their multi-dimensional aspect and activating the Hieros Gamos –

the inner alchemical marriage of the masculine and feminine energies within, and very skilfully identifying and removing all blocks that stand in the way of triumphant Twin Flame Union.

Jen has experienced huge breakthroughs recently due to working with very high-level mentors who are fully anchored in the millionaire mindset. This is having a huge impact on her working and her offerings that she has begun to share.

Visit Jen McCartys' Website Here

https://jenmccarty.co.uk/

SCAN ME

JOIN JEN'S SACRED COMMUNITIES ON SOCIAL MEDIA

Cosmicgypsy33 - Jen McCarty - LINKTREE WEBLINKS

www.linktr.ee/cosmicgypsy33

Official Jen McCarty - INSTAGRAM

www.instagram.com/officialjenmccarty144/

Jen McCarty23 - FACEBOOK

www.facebook.com/jen.mccarty23/

SCAN ME

By Jen McCarty

JOIN JEN'S SACRED COMMUNITIES ON SOCIAL MEDIA

The Event is Happening - FACEBOOK GROUP

www.facebook.com/groups/theeventishappening

SCAN ME

Cosmic Gypsy - Jen McCarty - YOUTUBE

www.youtube.com/channel/UC_8fJz5gAnhRqZ740Q
Xlzmw

SCAN ME

The Untended Altar

The altar is a vortex in our home, which is anchoring God's spiritual light in our space. The altar is a holy portal which truly can heal us.

In this powerful sacred, and potentially extremely life-changing book Jen McCarty shares the direct link between the internal altar and the external altar and how when we neglect our external altar, this has huge ramifications for us on a spiritual level.
Jen goes into great depth about the history of altars and how altars are used in many cultures, and she shares many potent ways to work with an altar, particularly using the five elements of earth air water fire and ether..
This book explains with profound clarity that an activated altar takes us out of the nightmare of secularism and places our consciousness back directly in the heart of divinity.

"This remarkable book, is doubtlessly the motivational kick up the backside I have been needing to get my house in order, and steer me forwards on my journey. "
Mairi Arthur
"This book Illuminates intention & awareness on levels unprecedented".
kristina

By Jen McCarty